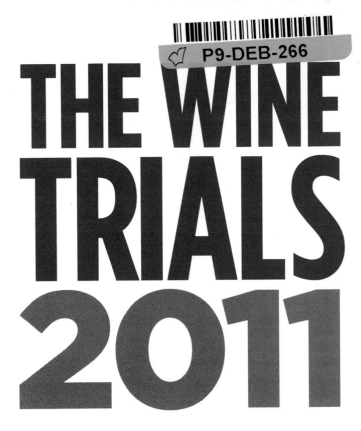

P9-DEB-266

# THE WINE TRIALS 2011

**Fearless Critic Media** New York

# Third edition, 2011

Printed in the United States of America

ISBN 978-1-6081601-6-7

10 9 8 7 6 5 4 3 2 1

## Other books now available from Fearless Critic Media

The Beer Trials: the essential guide to the world's most popular beers

Fearless Critic San Antonio Restaurant Guide
Fearless Critic Seattle Restaurant Guide
Fearless Critic Portland Restaurant Guide
Fearless Critic Washington DC Restaurant Guide
Fearless Critic Houston Restaurant Guide
Fearless Critic Austin Restaurant Guide
Fearless Critic New Haven Restaurant Guide

## Smartphone apps now or soon available from Fearless Critic Media

Fearless Critic restaurant guides for iPhone
Fearless Critic restaurant guides for Android

The Wine Trials for iPhone
The Wine Trials for Android

The Beer Trials for iPhone
The Beer Trials for Android

## On fearlesscritic.com

For everyone: restaurant guide content including sortable lists and ratings, what's open now, new reviews, and more

For subscribers: the entire text of Fearless Critic  restaurant guides

# Authors

**Robin Goldstein** is the founder and editor-in-chief of the Fearless Critic series, a contributing writer to the *New York Times* Freakonomics blog, and a visiting scholar in behavioral economics at the University of California, Berkeley, where he studies food and wine perception. He has authored six books of restaurant reviews and has written for more than 30 *Fodor's* travel guides, from Italy to Thailand, Argentina to Hong Kong. Robin is a graduate of Harvard University and the Yale Law School. He has a certificate in cooking from the French Culinary Institute in New York and a WSET advanced wine and spirits certificate.

**Alexis Herschkowitsch** is a co-author of five Fearless Critic restaurant guides. Alexis has written for the *Fodor's* travel guides to Mexico, Central America, and Thailand. She is a graduate of the University of Texas at Austin, and has a WSET advanced wine and spirits certificate.

**Tyce Walters** has created wine reviews from the notes of our editorial tasting panel for two editions of this guide. He is a student at the Yale Law School and a graduate of Yale University, where he founded the wine journal *Vino/Veritas: The Yale Wino*. He has also worked as a wine retail consultant and served as editor of the *Yale Philosophy Review*.

# Associate Editors

**Andrea Armeni** has practiced wine law in Napa Valley, taught sustainable development to oenologists in Paris, and currently lives in San Francisco, where he is a reporter for *Emerging Markets* magazine. Andrea is a graduate of Columbia University and the Yale Law School, and has contributed to numerous Fearless Critic food and wine books.

**Mark Walker** is the founder of the website WineLife365.com. WineLife365's commentary includes wine reviews (with a focus on wines costing less than $20), as well as other topics related to wine. Mark is a graduate of Widener University and has been studying wine for over 15 years.

# Editorial and blind tasting board

*The following people, listed alphabetically, served on our tasting panels and/or as editorial advisers. The opinions set forth in this book do not necessarily reflect the views of any of these individuals or their affiliated institutions. Any errors are ours alone.*

**Ellisa Cooper** is director of education for Barter House Wine Imports. **Brian DiMarco** is owner and president of Barter House Wine Imports and a graduate of the French Culinary Institute. **Julian Faulkner**, owner and winemaker of Le Grand Cros and Jules Wines in Côtes de Provence, has a master's degree in oenology from the École Nationale d'Ingénieurs des Travaux Agricoles de Bordeaux. **Alex Joerger** is currently the Director of Wine, Beer, and Spirits for Northeast-based Best Cellars and A&P stores. **Tracey Ellen Kamens** is Chief Education Officer of Grand Cru Classes in New York City. **Jake Katz** has a WSET advanced wine and spirits certificate and is a co-author of the article "Do More Expensive Wines Taste Better?". **Karen Man** is a graduate of the French Pastry School in Chicago and has cooked at the French Laundry restaurant in Yountville, California. **Erin McReynolds** is managing editor of the Fearless Critic Restaurant Guides, directing a national network of food critics and editing the series. **James Morrison** has been beverage director for the Fireman Hospitality Group and is currently a consultant for Barter House Wine Imports. **Stew Navarre** is a graduate of the Culinary Institute of America and has cooked at the Grove restaurant in Houston, Texas. **Benjamin Rosenblum** is an architect based in Berkeley, California, and has contributed to the *Fearless Critic New Haven Restaurant Guide*. **Karl Storchmann** is vice president of the American Association of Wine Economists, managing editor of the Journal of Wine Economics, and associate professor of economics at New York University. **Kent Wang** has been a staff member at the eGullet Society for Culinary Arts & Letters and has contributed to the *Fearless Critic Austin Restaurant Guide*. **Justin Yu** is a graduate of the Culinary Institute of America, has contributed to several Fearless Critic restaurant guides, and has cooked at Ubuntu restaurant in Napa, California.

# Scientific advisory board

*The following professors and scientists, listed alphabetically, offered their expertise to help interpret our results and review our methods and conclusions for scientific accuracy. The opinions set forth in this book do not necessarily reflect the views of any of these individuals or their affiliated institutions. Any errors are ours alone.*

# Other contributors

*The following people contributed generously to our project in numerous ways: organizing or hosting blind tastings, reviewing our methodology and conclusions, editing and proofreading drafts of the manuscript, and even hosting the authors in their homes. The opinions set forth in this book do not necessarily reflect the views of any of these individuals or their affiliated institutions. Any errors are ours alone.*

**Margarita Barcenas**, Event Coordinator
**Leah Barton**, Event Coordinator
**Hal Bayless**, Event Coordinator
**Nikia Bergan**, General Contributor
**Adam Brackman**, Photographer
**Bill Collins**, Event Host
**Daniel Frommer**, General Contributor
**James Frutkin**, Contributing Editor
**Andrew Gajkowski**, General Contributor
**Navid Ghedami**, Event Host
**Barry Goldstein**, Contributing Editor and Event Host
**Rosie Goldstein**, Event Host
**Kacie Gonzalez**, Publishing Assistant
**David Grossman**, Chef
**Claudio Guerra**, Event Host
**Candice Holden**, Event Host
**Rob Holden**, Event Host
**Daniel Horwitz**, Contributing Editor and Event Host
**Bobby Huegel**, Mixologist
**Roy Ip**, Chef and Event Host
**Winnie Ip**, Event Host
**Jeff Kaplan**, Event Coordinator
**Anat Kaufman**, Photographer
**David Kim**, Event Coordinator
**Sidney Kwiram**, Contributing Editor
**Duncan Levin**, Contributing Editor
**Benjamin Lima**, Contributing Editor
**Josh Loving**, Event Host
**Rebecca Markovits**, Contributing Editor

**Beth Martinez,** Event Host
**Dan Martinez,** Event Host
**Charles Mayes,** Event Host
**Colin McCarthy,** Event Coordinator
**Caroline McLean,** Event Host
**David Menschel,** Contributing Editor
**Clare Murumba,** Event Host
**Angie Niles,** Event Coordinator
**Justin Nowell,** Video Editor
**Coco Owens,** Publishing Assistant
**Brane Poledica,** Event Host
**Isaure de Pontbriand,** Contributing Editor
**Karisa Prestera,** Event Host
**Daniel Rosenblum,** Photographer
**Abigail Roth,** Event Coordinator
**James Saccento,** General Contributor
**Marcus Samuelsson,** Chef and Event Host
**Claude Solliard,** Chef and Event Host
**Kelly Stecker,** Publishing Assistant and Photographer
**Brian Stubbs,** Event Host
**Harold Stubbs,** Contributing Editor
**Lu Stubbs,** Contributing Editor
**Susan Stubbs,** Contributing Editor and Event Host
**Cody Taylor,** Event Coordinator
**Mark Trachtenberg,** Event Host
**Darya Trapeznikova,** Event Coordinator
**Andy Vickery,** Event Host
**Carol Vickery,** Event Host
**Kristi Walker,** Event Host
**Mark Walker,** Event Host

We would also like to thank the following restaurants for hosting events and wine tastings for *The Wine Trials*:

**Aquavit**, New York, NY

**Bella's**, New York, NY

**Bistro Lancaster**, Houston, TX

**Bistro Les Gras**, Northampton, MA

**Café Josie**, Austin, TX

**Fino**, Austin, TX

**Paradise City Tavern**, Northampton, MA

**Le Petit Café**, Branford, CT

**Lotus**, New York, NY

**Seppi's**, New York, NY

**Upstairs on the Square**, Cambridge, MA

# Experimental blind tasters

*The following people participated in the 2008 blind-tasting experiment that formed the empirical basis for the paper "Do More Expensive Wines Taste Better?" and the framework for the first portion of this book. The opinions set forth in this book do not necessarily reflect the views of any of these individuals. Any errors are ours alone.*

Ned Adamson, Susan Adamson, Suzanne Adelman, Caroline Adler, Bob Agoglia, Ali Ahsan, Frances Aldous-Worley, Elnaz Alipour-Assiabi, Johan Almenberg, Anna Dreber Almenberg, Jessica Amato, Michael Amendola, Janelle Anderson, Whitney Angstadt, Lorenzo Aragona, Fernando Aramburo, Larinia Arena, David L. Ash, Brenda Audino, Laura Austin, Marty Austin, Leila Ayachi, Leigh M. Bailey, Donna L. Balin, Scott A. Balin, David Ball, Nicole Ball, Oleg Balter, Shai Bandner, Pat Barbro, Margarita Barcenas, Rhondale-Marie Barras, Michael Barron, Catherine Barry, Ryan Barry, Leah Barton, Louise Barton, Ran Barton, Ben Batchelder, Anne C. Bauer, Nathaniel Baum-Snow, Hal Bayless, Andrew Benner, Zachary Bennett, Steven Bercu, Amber Berend, Edward H. Berman, Julia Berman, Jason Berns, Jennifer Berns, Susan Biancani, Chris Black, J.D. Bloodworth, Rayna Bourke, Vanessa Treviño Boyd, Kathleen Boyle, Wood Boyles, Adam Brackman, Uda M. Bradford, Delana Brandon, Benjamin J. Brandow, Kevin Brass, Lietza Brass, Judith Brock, Patrick Brock, Stacey Brock, Aileen B. Brophy, Ezra T. Brown, Jaclynn T. Brown, Joy Brunner, L.R. Brunner, S.S. Brunner, Robert Buchele, Thomas Burke, Gary L. Bush, Nancy H. Bush, Matthew J. Caballero, Mark Cabell, Rick Cagney, Michele Camp, Jeff Caplan, Lisa Carley, Ale Carlos, Robert Carroll, Benjamin Carter, Katharine Carter, Kimberly Casey, Marlon Castillo, Matt Cerimele, Claire Champagne, John Champagne, Zoe Chance, Benjamin Chang, Helen Chong, Gaetan Ciampini, Dennis Clark, Joanna Cline, John B. Clutterbuck, Suzanna Cole, Patty Collins, William M. Collins, Marcus Allen Cooper, Russell W. Cooper, David Cordúa, Denis Costaz, Nadia Croes, Katy Cuddihee, Marc Cuenod, Martha Cuenod, Jessica Czerwin, Nat Davis, C.J. Dean, Frank Debons, Jana Demetral, Nisha Desai, Brian DiMarco, Shoshana Dobrow, Chezmin

## Experimental blind tasters *continued*

N. Dolinsky, Jed Dooley, Susan K. Dudek, Shaun Duffy, Carol Duke, Seth Dunn, Kenneth Dyer, Julie Sinclair Eakin, James Endicott, Joel Ephross, Matt Epstein, Sarah Escobar, Samantha Essen, Julie Fairbanks, Virginia H. Fallon, Julian Faulkner, Silvio Ferrari, Amy E. Ferrer, Monica Fields, Ben Fieman, Cristina Finan, Paul Flores, Sharla Flores, Jeff Flynn, Marcy Flynn, Christine Folch, Eric Foret, Ana Fox, Judd Frankel, Shane Frederick, John Freeman, Linda Freeman, Sylvia Freeman, Morgan Friedman, Marika Frumes, Jim Frutkin, Eleni Gage, Andrew Gajkowski, Jessica L. Gant, Seanna Garrison, Thomas J. Garza, Ellen Gay, Marva Gay, Robert Gerstle, Jeffrey Giles, James A. Gleason, Julie Goldman, Barry Goldstein, Valerie Golin, Maria J. Gomez, Nick Gossett, Amy Grande, Michelle Grasso, Ed Greenbaum, Claire Liu Greenberg, Seth Grossman, Frederic Guarino, Elaine Gubbins, Megan G. Gubbins, Claudio Guerra, Elisabeth Gutowski, John Ha, Casey Dué Hackney, Ryan Hackney, Lauren Hale, Deb Hall, William Erin Hall, Mike Handel, Tracie Handel, Michelle S. Hardy, Joan Harmon, Amy K. Harper, Elizabeth W. Harries, Brian Hay, Monica Hayes, Kristen Hendricks, Jodie Hermann, David Hesse, Leslie Hill, Ed Hirs, Steven Hite, Tim Tix, Candice Holden, David Holden, Meg Parker Holden, Stacey Holman, Ellen Horne, Pamela Horton, Daniel Horwitz, Jenny Howe, Lee-Sean Huang, Tasneem Husain, Alexandra Hynes, Roy Ip, Reena Isaac, Karen G. Jackson, Tim Jensen, Beverly Jernigan, Josean Jimenez, Alexis Johnson, Gary Johnson, Gita Joshua, Ali Jouzdani, Eirini Kaissaratou, Jeff Kaplan, Laurence A. Kaplan, Jake Katz, Michael G. Katz, Anat Kaufman, Alexandra Kaufmann, Sarah Kelly, Emily Kelsch, Samantha Kennedy, Fred Kilehorn, Nina Kiernan, David Kim, Allison Kirby, Lauren Klein, Sarah K. Kozlowski, Alison Kriviskey, Bruce M. Kriviskey, Tim Kutach, Lance Lahr, Dea Larson, Nichole Byrne Lau, Samantha Lazarus, Eugene Lee, Risha Lee, Jennifer A. Lee, Kari Leeper, Amelia Lester, Michael Levi, Duncan Levin, Steve Levine, Benjamin Lima, Kristin Lindner, Jes Logan, Matthew Lombardi, Stephen G. Long, Ayanna Lonian, Natalie Louie, Josh Loving, Ginger Lowry, Jennifer Luddy, Kerry Lusignan, Jane Baxter Lynn, Zachary Mallavia, Will Manlove, Edward T. Mannix, III, Paul A. Mardas, Olga Gonzalez Marruffo, Andrea Marsh, Jonathan Martel, Moira Bessette Martin, Thomas Martin, Dan Martinez, Beth Martinez, Tom McCasland, Lindsey

## Experimental blind tasters *continued*

McCormack, Sally McDaniel, Caroline McLean, Megan McMahon, Walter J. McMahon, James NcNair, Erin McReynolds, Michael Macedo Meazell, Elsa Mehary, Ferne Mele, David Mench, David Menschel, Elizabeth Merrill, Christiane Metral, Charles H. Michelet, George I. Miller, Jaclyn Miller, Samantha Miller, Julie Mischlich, Tejal Mody, Dorothy Molnar, Amy E. Moran, Jamie Lynn Morgan, Steven R. Moscoe, Chris Mrema, Matthias Mueller, Clare Kogire Murumba, Luke Murumba, Keren Murumba, Matthew Murumba, Samuel Murumba, Vinay B. Nair, Joe Napolitano, Stew Navarre, Daniel Nelson, Monika Powe Nelson, Catherine New, Martin A. Nowak, Justin Nowell, Thomas Nowell, Louis Orenstein, Anne Ouimette, Debbie Padon, Tom Pappalardo, William Parra, Lisa Parrish, Akshay Patil, Drew Patterson, Elizabeth Morrison Petegorsky, Stephen Petegorsky, Isaure de Pontbriand, Charles B. Powers, Ron Prashker, Jennie Pries, Risher Randall, Andrea Ranft, Greg Ranft, Ofir Reichenberg, Taj Reid, Julee Resendez, George Reynolds, Mark Reynolds, Elizabeth Richmond-Garza, Matt Rigney, Bob A. Rivollier, Don Robbins, Bill Roberts, Gerrit Rogers, Medora M. Rogers, Patrick Rohan, Kayla Rosenberg, Benjamin Rosenblum, Daniel Rosenblum, Murry Rosenblum, Debbie Rosmarin, Jori Ross, Elizabeth A. Rovere, Mary Pat Roy, Michael J. Roy, Denise Ruhl, James Saccento, Kate Drake Saccento, Jane Sackett, Sarah Salinas, M. Melinda Sanders, Sherri Sandifer, Susan Sandikcioglu, Jorge Sanhueza-Lyon, Ruben Sanz Ramiro, Sue Schmidt, Tatiana Schnur, Peter Schultz, Joseph A. Sena, Jr., Taylor Senatore, Larry Shielerran, Rachel Shiffrin, Erin Sibley, Jeff Siegel, Leslie Silbert, Will Silverman, Mark Simmelkjaes, Emily Singer, Alison D. Smith, Sarah Smith, Michael Sobolevsky, John P. Sobolweski, Claude A. Solliard, Patricia Sophy-McNair, Linda K. Sparks, Joel Spiro, Ashley St. Clair, Chanel Eve Stark, Kelly Stecker, Judith Stinson, Robert C. Stinson, Brian Stubbs, Sue Stubbs, Kari Sullivan, Marty Sullivan, Linda Summers, Sara Jane Summers, Adam Taplin, Laura Tatum, Cody Taylor, Mary Taylor, Andrew Teich, Antonia Thomas, Elana Thurston-Milgrom, Melissa Tischler, Eric Titner, Anne Todd, Bruce Tolda, Darya Trapeznikova, Cynthia Urrutia, Justin Vann, Holly M. Veech, Alan Verson, Matt Verson, Paula Verson, A. Vora, Preeya Vyas, Johannes Walker, Kristi Walker, Linda Walker, Brad Wall, Ruth Waser, Jillian Wein, Thomas Weiner, Andrew Whitcomb, Kirk Wickline, Cynthia M. Williams,

## Experimental blind tasters *continued*

Margot Williams, Lisa Michelle Wilmore, Elsie E. Wilmoth, Rae Wilson, Clarence Wine, Matt Wong, Betty Yip, Randy Yost, Richard Young, Justin Yu, Vadim Zhitomirsky, George R. Zimmerman, Donald H. Zuckerman, Donna E. Zuckerman, Monwabisi Zukani

# Contents

# Preface to the new 2011 edition

Today is a good day to be a wine drinker in North America. Those of us who drink wine, whether every night or only on the most special of occasions, currently have access to bottles from a dizzying array of countries and regions. For the first time, wine recently surpassed beer as the preferred alcoholic beverage of American drinkers. And the renewed attention to value wines—a small silver lining of the recent recession—shows no signs of abating.

Above all, we can take pride in the stunning diversity of today's wine offerings. Just a few years ago the mainstream American wine scene seemed destined to become the vinous equivalent of a strip mall, with an unending—and indistinguishable—parade of homogenous "international" wines. Stuffed with oak and jammy fruit, and perhaps featuring an adorable critter on the label, these wines multiplied so rapidly that they threatened to squeeze out small producers from shelves. And whether you love or detest critter wines stylistically, the loss of diversity in the wine world is worth lamenting.

Thankfully, Americans have been fighting back. A growing number of drinkers have begun to embrace blind tasting and fully trust their own palates, to patronize smaller retailers passionate about the wines they sell, to test their boundaries and to seek out new and exciting producers.

All these efforts have created some results. Intimate, artisanal wine stores are flourishing in cities from New York to Topeka; wines from small countries and smaller producers can increasingly be found even in corner liquor stores and casual restaurants. Our selections reflect this diversity, with wines from Bulgaria, Turkey, Spain, and Portugal joining the usual suspects among our blind taster favorites. Gewürztraminer and Vinho Verde may not be household names yet, but they're no longer suspiciously foreign either. In fact, you might be able to find one of these wines at your local supermarket.

But it is too early for self-congratulation. Yellow Tail and its kin still dominate the value-seeking wine market, while "lifestyle brands" like Veuve Clicquot and Dom Pérignon (owned by the massive luxury goods corporation Louis Vuitton Moët Hennessy) pitch their advertising to a more aspirational demographic. And while several highly commercial wines are featured in these pages, the sad fact remains that the business model of most of the large-scale wine factories depends more on branding, advertising, price signaling, and other controls on consumption norms than on great winemaking. Like it or not, these wines are being marketed with a method once reserved for fashion and cosmetics: by selling an image, a lifestyle, a place in the social world.

Yet our blind tastings have shown, again and again, that people consistently prefer a $9 Spanish Cava to that $40 Veuve—and even to a $150 Dom Pérignon. In fact, when we served 6,000 wines hidden in brown paper bags to more than 500 people—a large-scale experiment on a diverse mix of wine experts and everyday wine drinkers—we found that, on the whole, people actually preferred the cheaper wines to the more expensive wines. It is only by blind tasting and learning to trust our individual palates that we can cut through the haze of marketing to discover the wines we truly like. And in doing so, our individual tastes will ensure the continued diversity of the wine world itself.

Part I of this book—the "blind tasting manifesto"—discusses our blind tasting results in light of some of the most cutting-edge work in behavioral economics and neuroscience. Whether or not you're a wine expert, we aim to challenge some of your most basic assumptions about wine, and to encourage you to question the orthodoxy that governs wine pricing and wine ratings. New to this edition is chapter 8, which reviews the newest scientific research on wine perception since the publication of our last edition, *Wine Trials 2010*.

Part II—the 2011 Wine Trials themselves—aims to help you better navigate the inexpensive wine shelf. Here, we reveal and review 175 winning wines under $15 that outscored $50 to $150 bottles in a series of rigorous brown-bag blind tasting tastings conducted by our editors this year.

Once again, we reviewed an entirely new lineup of wines, and once again we increased the number of bottles included—this time to 175. We also further lowered our production minimum for inclusion in the book, from 20,000 cases of wine to 10,000.[1] This number allowed us to include smaller, more artisanal producers while still ensuring that most of the wines are nationally distributed and easy to acquire. We continued to employ a nomination system for the selection of wines to be tasted: we have accepted nominations and submissions from professionals in many different areas of the wine industry, from producers to sommeliers, importers to retailers, creating an initial selection of the more than 500 widely available wines under $15 that people within the industry like best.

The second phase—the blind tastings themselves—narrowed the pool again by more than two-thirds, to the 175 *Wine Trials* winners presented in Part II. Each of these wines outscored more expensive bottles in our brown-bag blind tastings. We think that the result is a rich, diverse, carefully chosen pool of wines that will bring you some of the best pleasure-to-dollar ratios on the market. Every wine in the book is recommended as one of the best widely available values under $15, beating out hundreds of other carefully chosen wines that did not meet the bar. We have not rated wines numerically in this book, but we did want to bestow awards upon the wines that did the very best in our tastings. We therefore chose a set of finalists—the wines our editors liked best in the first round of blind tastings—and we held a playoff blind tasting in which we selected a winner in each of our style categories.

None of the tasting results from our last edition were counted for this edition; every wine tasted in the 2011 trials has been newly released since the first edition. The 55 repeat winners in *The Wine Trials 2011* each represent a new release or new vintage of the wine that won in the previous edition. Of course, that also means that quite a few previous winners *didn't* make this year's top 175.

There is a commonly held belief that inexpensive wines don't tend to change much from year to year. This is a myth. Indeed, due to lower budgets and a narrower range of winemaking techniques, small-production wineries might even be *more* sensitive to the vagaries of weather.

Just as importantly, many of these wines change stylistically from vintage to vintage as a result of winemaker choices: how much oak is used, whether grapes are harvested late to increase jammy flavors, whether to retain sugar, etc. These differences can be dramatic, with a Chardonnay that tasted clean and fruity one year seeming fat, rich, and oaky the next. Such phenomena, along with the thousands of new bottles put onto the market every year, make it absolutely crucial for us to release a new edition of *The Wine Trials* annually.

While Part II may be more useful as a buying guide, we hope you will take the time to read and engage with the ideas in Part I as well. There has been a great deal of debate in the wine world surrounding this book, but we think one fact is incontestable: the more we learn to trust our palates and discover which wines, styles, and regions we truly like (rather than which ones the wine industry says we should like), the better off we'll be as drinkers. So don't be too surprised if your preferences, even as they become more sophisticated, never turn out to match up well to the hierarchical structure that currently dominates the industry. The most important point of all is to take our thoughts and recommendations as starting points, not endpoints; to blind taste yourself; and to write to the authors at fearless@fearlesscritic.com if you would like to comment on anything we have to say.

There are a host of factors—social, psychological, and informational—blocking the path to discovering our personal wine preferences. Within these pages we hope to provide a guide to navigating those obstacles. We aim to be useful as a tool that will encourage you to trust your palate more and wine marketing less, and that will help you spend your money on wines whose fundamental properties you truly enjoy rather than ones you think you should enjoy. In doing so, we're confident that you'll drink even better and contribute even more to the astounding diversity of today's wine world.

**Part I** The blind tasting manifesto
*by Robin Goldstein*

# Chapter 1 Blind taste

Dom Pérignon, a $150 Champagne from France, and Domaine Ste. Michelle Cuvée Brut, a $12 sparkling wine from Washington State, are both made in the traditional Champagne method. Both wines are widely available at wine stores, liquor stores, and restaurants. Both are dry, with high acidity. The two bottles are more or less the same size and shape. So why are consumers willing to pay more than 12 times more for one than for the other?

The most obvious explanation would be that, to most wine drinkers, the liquid inside the bottle of Dom Pérignon tastes better than the liquid inside the bottle of Domaine Ste. Michelle—if not 12 times better, then at least somewhat better.[2] However, that doesn't seem to be the case. Between fall 2007 and spring 2008, we conducted an experiment serving these two sparkling wines head-to-head in five different blind tastings, with the bottles hidden inside brown paper bags. And 41 of 62 tasters—about two thirds—preferred the Domaine Ste. Michelle.

In October 2009, we replicated this experiment on a smaller scale with newer releases of the two sparkling wines. This time, we served them to a group of professional chefs, certified sommeliers, and food writers, of which more than 70% preferred the humble $12 bottle to the famous $150 one. This time, we also threw in Veuve Clicquot, a popular $40 Champagne from the same luxury products group—LVMH—that makes Dom Pérignon. More than 85% of tasters preferred the Domaine Ste. Michelle to the Veuve. This doesn't seem to be a single, idiosyncratic instance in which people's tastes happen to run contrary to popular wisdom or market prices. The Champagne battle described above was just a small part of a series of blind tastings that we conducted around the country over that same time span. It was an experiment in which we poured more than 6,000 glasses of wine from brown-bagged bottles that cost from $1.50 to $150.

The result? As a whole, the group actually preferred the cheaper wines to the more expensive wines—by a statistically significant margin.

The 507 blind tasters in this 2007–2008 experiment represented many different segments of the wine-buying world. They were professionals in a wide range of fields. Some were wine experts, others everyday wine drinkers. They included New York City sommeliers and Harvard professors, winemakers from France, neuroscientists and artists, top chefs and college students, doctors and lawyers, wine importers and wine store owners, novelists and economists, TV comedy writers and oenologists, bartenders and grad students, 21-year-olds and 88-year-olds, socialists and conservatives, heavy drinkers and lightweights.

On the whole, tasters preferred a (then-)nine-dollar Beringer Founders' Estate Cabernet Sauvignon to a $120 wine from the same grape and the same producer: Beringer Private Reserve Cabernet Sauvignon. They preferred a six-dollar Vinho Verde from Portugal to a $40 Cakebread Chardonnay and a $50 Chassagne-Montrachet 1er Cru from Louis Latour. And when we concealed the labels and prices of 27 sparkling wines and asked people to rate them, the Dom Pérignon finished 17th—behind 14 sparkling wines that cost less than $15, eight of which cost less than $10.[3]

Does this mean that the $12 Domaine Ste. Michelle is objectively better than the $150 bottle of Dom? In an abstract, Platonic sense—or by established industry norms—perhaps not. In fact, the wine experts among our tasters didn't dislike the expensive wines in the way that everyday wine drinkers did; they liked more expensive wines as much, or even a bit more, than cheaper wines (although they still didn't like the Dom better than the Domaine Ste. Michelle).

But the vast majority of wine consumers are everyday wine drinkers, not experts. At a minimum, it seems clear that many Americans might be wasting at least $138, at least where taste is concerned, when they buy Dom Pérignon for special occasions. There is a mounting body of evidence from within and without the wine world that wine pricing is more arbitrary than one might assume, but ours was one of the first studies to show an inverse correlation between price and preference. That inverse correlation was moderate but statistically significant across all of our tasters ($p=0.038$; this means that there was only a 3.8% probability that our results came about by chance—in the sciences, the generally accepted standard for statistical significance is a p-value of less than 0.05). When you exclude the very cheapest and most expensive wines and just look at the mid-range wines—those priced between $6 and $15—the effect is even stronger ($p=0.004$).[4]

We did not allow the tasters to discuss the wines with each other before rating them, and we kept the wines concealed in their numbered brown paper bags until after the evaluation forms had been turned in. In order to weigh the results of consistent tasters more than inconsistent tasters, we subjected people to the "twin-wine test," serving them two identical wines in the same flight of six—unbeknownst to the tasters, of course. With the help of our statistics team, we gave less weight to the opinions of tasters who rated the identical wines differently.

The results of our experiment are explained in technical form in the appendix, written by economists Johan Almenberg and Anna Dreber Almenberg, and they are also presented in an academic paper that we published in the Journal of Wine Economics entitled "Do More Expensive Wines Taste Better?".[5]

By no means are all wine critics and commentators in denial of this effect. Many have commented on the arbitrariness of pricing, including Master of Wine Jancis Robinson, one of the world's foremost wine writers, who has observed a "lack of correlation between price and pleasure." She writes: "Perhaps it is not so surprising that a first-rate example of a little-known wine can seem much more memorable than something more famous selling at ten times the price…What is more extraordinary is the wild price variation at the very top end. Demand bubbles up mysteriously, apparently fuelled by fashion and rumour as much as by intrinsic quality."[6]

In their seminal 1976 book on wine quality measurement, *Wines: Their Sensory Evaluation*, UC Davis professors Maynard Amerine (an oenologist) and Edward Roessler (a mathematician) tend to concur, although they, like Robinson, focus on the overpricing of super-premium wines: "[P]rice depends on many factors that are not necessarily related to quality. Those who buy wines on a price basis deserve what they get. ... Some famous vineyards, secure in the knowledge that they have an established market, often charge whatever the market will bear."[7]

Between 1997 and 2001, researchers Sébastien Lecocq and Michael Visser conducted three large-scale expert blind tastings of a total of 1,409 wines from Bordeaux and Burgundy under highly controlled conditions with professional tasters from the Institut National de la Consommation. They found that the tasters' sensory evaluations of the wines were only very weakly correlated with price, leading Lecocq and Visser to conclude that "the market price of Bordeaux wine can be explained primarily by the objective characteristics appearing on the label of the bottle."

Those tastings involved only experts, but Lecocq and Visser foreshadow our results with everyday wine drinkers when they suggest that "when non-experts blind-taste cheap and expensive wines they typically tend to prefer the cheaper ones."[8]

In a series of blind tastings conducted by Hilke Plassmann, Antonio Rangel, and their colleagues at Stanford Business School and Cal Tech—part of an important brain-scanning study that I'll come back to in chapter 2—everyday wine drinkers rated the cheap wines higher than they rated the expensive wines, just as they did in our blind tastings. And in an experiment conducted by Roman Weil, which will be discussed in chapter 3, everyday wine drinkers didn't prefer reserve wines to regular wines, even though the wines differed in price by an order of magnitude.

Lecocq and Visser themselves foreshadowed these results. While their extensive tastings of Bordeaux and Burgundy wines only involved experts, they suggested that "when non-experts blind-taste cheap and expensive wines they typically tend to prefer the cheaper ones."

Our observations, like those of the scholars above, could hardly contrast any more starkly with the patterns of wine ratings on the 100-point scales used by magazine critics, which tend to track wine prices consistently (see chapter 3 for evidence of that).

What is going on here? If blind tasting experiments show that wine pricing is arbitrary from the perspective of everyday wine drinkers, then why are the magazine ratings that those drinkers rely on so directly correlated with price? And why do everyday wine drinkers still trust those ratings, and spend money on expensive wine?

# Chapter 2 The taste of money

Moët & Chandon, the producer of Dom Pérignon, sells more than 60 million bottles of premium-priced Champagne every year—most of them to everyday wine drinkers, not wine professionals. Putting aside our results for a moment, it's hard to imagine that millions of consumers would be buying $30 to $150 Champagnes and really, truly enjoying them less than $10 sparkling wines. Most of those people must feel, at least, that they're getting their money's worth; otherwise, presumably, they wouldn't keep buying expensive Champagne.[9]

The sheer number of amateur wine bloggers on the Internet at the moment, many of whom spend hours every day writing extensive reviews for no pay, seems evidence enough to demonstrate wine lovers' passionate enjoyment of expensive wine. It would seem ludicrous to suggest that amateur wine lovers are not really enjoying their $2,000 bottles of Château Margaux or Screaming Eagle, or to suspect their passion to be anything less than genuine. Yet even that passion seems to conflict with our results—and with the results of scientists in wine economics and cognition.

What do we make, for instance, of the work of wine researcher Frédéric Brochet, who fooled 57 French wine experts by serving them two identical wines, one in an expensive Grand Cru bottle, the other in a cheap Vin de Table bottle? Although both bottles contained the same wine—a mid-range Bordeaux—Brochet's subjects preferred the wine from the Grand Cru bottle by a dramatic margin. They used positive terms like "excellent," "good," "complex," and "long" more than twice as often when describing the supposed Grand Cru as they did when describing the supposed Vin de Table, and, conversely, used negative terms like "unbalanced," "short," "flat," and "simple" more than twice as much when describing the supposed Vin de Table.

Another of Brochet's experiments showed that, like price, the color of a wine can affect subjects' reported experiences. When 54 subjects tasted a white wine under normal conditions, they tended to use typical white-wine descriptors (e.g. "fresh," "lemon," "apricot," and "honey") to describe their experience. But when they tasted that same white wine colored with a flavorless dye to look like red wine, the tasters switched to typical red-wine descriptors (e.g. "red currant," "cherry," "raspberry," and "spice"). The influence of the wine's color on their taste experience, or at least their judgment, was profound.[10]

A couple of decades earlier, in *Wines: Their Sensory Evaluation*, Amerine and Roessler anticipate Brochet's results: "It is surprising," they write, "how many so-called wine experts are 'label drinkers.' Their sensory judgment is based on the source or reputation of the wine, or its producer, or the year of production."

But what do they mean by "sensory judgment"? Is it wine drinkers' judgment of the experience that's altered by the knowledge that a wine is expensive, or is it the experience itself?

I believe it to be the latter: it's the experience itself that changes once you know the wine is expensive. I do not believe that most wine drinkers simply pretend to like wine better because it's expensive, and I do not believe that they are lying to others, or even to themselves, when they report getting more pleasure from premium-priced wine.

I believe that wine actually tastes better when you know it's expensive, in every meaningful sense of the word "taste." For wine as for medicine, the placebo effect is not a mere delusion; it is a physical reality. The experience of sipping a wine you know to be expensive, then, is a real taste experience. It is the taste of money.

The best evidence that the placebo effect can change the experience of drinking itself comes from an article co-authored by

Shane Frederick, Dan Ariely, and Leonard Lee. It's a study about beer.

First, some background about experimental beer perception work: in 1964, it had been shown that beer drinkers, under experimental conditions, didn't prefer their favorite beers in blind tastings when the labels were hidden. In fact, they couldn't even reliably distinguish between different brands of pale lager beer.[11] In 2009, my co-author Seamus Campbell and I reached a similar result when we served three different European pale lager beers—Heineken, Stella, and Czechvar—to 138 regular beer drinkers in Portland, Oregon, and they did no better than chance at determining which two beers in a group of three were identical.[12]

Frederick and Ariely, who were interested in pinning down the precise moment at which sensory experience was shaped and preferences formed, ran a complex experiment that involved adding balsamic vinegar to beer before serving it. Here's how it worked: 388 tasters were randomly assigned to three different groups. The first group of tasters rated both beers—with and without vinegar—with no information about the ingredients, and 59% of them preferred the beer with vinegar (apparently, for many people, balsamic vinegar can improve the taste of beer). Tasters in the second group were instead informed of the ingredients before tasting; of that group, only 30% preferred the beer with vinegar. Their negative expectations seem to have colored their experience and reduced the pleasure they got from drinking the vinegared beer. Most interesting, however, were the tasters in the third group, who were told about the vinegar after tasting it, but before rating it. That group, like the first group, preferred the vinegared beer—even though they knew it contained vinegar before assigning their ratings. The first and third groups did not differ significantly in their preferences.[13]

The punch line is that the knowledge that there was vinegar in the beer affected people's taste experience if they were told about it beforehand, but it didn't significantly change their judgment of the beer after they'd already tasted. To me, this is strong evidence that expectations exert more influence on the level of taste experience than they do on the level of taste judgment.

One of the most talked-about wine articles in years has come from Hilke Plassmann, Antonio Rangel, and their colleagues at Stanford Business School and the California Institute of Technology, who added a set of fMRI brain-scan results to this remarkable body of evidence.[14] fMRI—short for functional magnetic resonance imaging—is a brain-scanning technology that (roughly speaking) measures changes in blood flow to different parts of the brain over time. There are some major drawbacks to the technique; for instance, subjects must lie very still inside a cylinder, which is obviously a bit different from the way we normally enjoy wine. More importantly, subjects in fMRI experiments have to sip liquids from a tube—so they don't get to swirl and smell the wine.

Still, Plassmann and Rangel's results are fascinating. In their experiment, 20 subjects in fMRI machines were told that they would taste five different Cabernet Sauvignon wines whose retail prices were $5, $10, $35, $45, and $90. In reality, the subjects were only served three wines: a $5 wine, a $45 wine, and a $90 wine. They were served the $5 wine twice, once while being told it cost $45 and once while being told its real cost. Likewise, they were served the $90 wine twice, once while being told it cost $10.

If you've read up to this point in the book, you probably won't be surprised by what happened: subjects' preferences correlated with the fake prices of the wines, not with the actual prices. When people thought they were drinking $90 wine, they loved it, even if it was actually $10 wine. What's more, blood flow to a brain area commonly associated with pleasure—the left medial orbitofrontal cortex—also was correlated with the fake price of the wines, but not with the actual price. For the first time, the neural correlates of price expectations creating pleasure were visible.

In a footnote to their study, Plassmann and Rangel had their subjects taste the same wines a few weeks later during a "post-experimental session without price cues"—that is, a straight-up blind tasting. And in that tasting, subjects actually preferred the $5 wine to the $90 wine. Sound familiar?

The wine placebo effect is real. We must accept that truth about ourselves. It doesn't mean that wine aficionados and experts are con artists, nor does it mean that people don't legitimately sense pleasurable qualities in very expensive wine, even when they taste it blind. But it does mean that when we don't taste blind, it's almost impossible to know whether the pleasure of expensive wine is coming from its own taste, or from the taste of money.

# Chapter 3 The perfect palate?

From 2000 to 2007, *Wine Spectator* rated 6,475 wines that cost $10 or less. Of those, only three of them—four hundredths of one percent—scored above 90 on the magazine's 100-point scale, and none scored above 91. By comparison, for those same vintages, of the 2,490 wines reviewed in *Wine Spectator* that cost $100 or more, 1,781 of them—more than 71%—scored above 90. *Wine Enthusiast* tells a similar story: of the 5,896 wines from the 2000 to 2007 vintages listed at $10 or less in their database, only two scored above 91.[15]

Could these numbers really reflect the tasters' experiences? Taste and smell, the so-called "chemical senses," are the most fickle and least quantifiable of our sensory systems. When people rate tastes and smells, the variance in their results tends to be extraordinarily high, even in the most controlled of cognitive tests. And wine is one of the most volatile organic substances that we ingest.

Considering wine's high sensitivity to oxygen, to temperature, and to time—complicated further by the physical unpredictability of our palates—the degree of correlation between price and qualitative score in the mainstream wine publications has become harder and harder to accept with each additional scientific study published on the subject. How could our results diverge so dramatically from the magazine critics' opinions?

Let's put aside, for a moment, the implausibility of the notion that *Wine Spectator*'s price-score correlation could have occurred naturally under controlled blind tasting conditions with any tasters. The most obvious explanation for this disconnect would then be that expensive wine is simply an acquired taste, and that the vast majority of wine drinkers—like the subjects of the experiments cited above, including ours—just haven't acquired that taste the way that these elite tasters have. Perhaps the magazines have cornered the market on critics who have "perfect palates"—the rare ability to taste something totally different in these expensive wines, something that simply could not exist in a $10 bottle. Maybe it's something that amateur wine drinkers, and even many wine experts, just can't detect, or—alternatively—can detect, but dislike.

Roman Weil, a professor of accounting at the University of Chicago, has shown that non-experts' preferences seem to have little do to with experts' ratings. In a fascinating study, he served blind tastes of the same wine from two different vintages, one that had been deemed "good" by wine experts, the other deemed "bad." Tasters also compared a prestigious reserve bottling against a regular bottling, again blind. In both cases, the tasters didn't do much better than chance at telling the two wines apart, and even when they did, they were as likely to prefer the cheap bottle as the expensive bottle—even though, in both cases, the prices differed by an order of magnitude. So for Weil's everyday wine drinkers, choosing the wines lauded by the critics didn't translate to any additional pleasure—when they tasted blind, of course.[16]

Weil did not administer his test to wine experts, but there is evidence that experts and everyday wine drinkers do have different taste in wine. Within the subset of wine experts in our blind tastings, there was a slight positive correlation—rather than a negative one—between price and preference. Still, the effect was only marginally significant, and our experts' opinions were nowhere near as price-correlated as are those of the *Wine Spectator* critics'. Neither were the opinions of Lecocq and Visser's wine experts. In fact, to my knowledge, no scientific blind-tasting study of wine experts has ever shown expensive wines to do as consistently well, or cheap wines to do as consistently poorly, as they do in *Wine Spectator*.

There is one particularly compelling recent piece of evidence that wine experts' results, like the results from non-experts, might be characterized more by inconsistency than by consistency. It comes from Robert Hodgson, a retired oceanography and statistics professor who also runs a small winery called Fieldbrook in Humboldt County, a region better known for other crops.

For years, like other small winemakers looking for ways to distinguish their wines from the competition, Hodgson would submit his wines to various medal competitions in California and elsewhere. But the results seemed to have no pattern at all. At one competition, one wine would win a gold medal, while another would win no medal at all; at another competition, the results were precisely reversed.

The judges at these competitions were experts in the field—winemakers, oenologists, wine writers, and such. Yet the more competitions Hodgson entered, the more suspicious he became that the results were coming out more or less random, and that the best way to win medals was not to make the best wine possible, but rather to simply enter as many competitions as possible.

Testing that hypothesis, though, proved to be a difficult task. The problem was that while information about which wines won medals is readily accessible, information about which wines entered but didn't win is much harder to come by. After a lot of searching, Hodgson finally found what he was looking for in a complex data set of more than 4,000 entries into 13 U.S. wine competitions in 2003.

Hodgson's analysis, published in the *Journal of Wine Economics* in spring 2009, investigated the degree of consistency between expert judges' blind-tasting ratings of the same wines in different competitions. His evidence indicated that "[there is] almost no consensus among the 13 wine competitions regarding wine quality"; that "for wines receiving a gold medal in one or more competitions, it is very likely that the same wine received no award at another"; and that "the likelihood of receiving a gold medal can be statistically explained by chance alone." A newer study by Hodgson on individual judge reliability rating the same wine more than once—described in greater depth in chapter 8, "New Experimental Results"—showed that only 10% of wine fair judges were "consistently consistent," that is, consistently assigned the same wine to the same medal range when tasting it more than once.

When anyone—even a top wine expert—assigns a numerical rating to wine, even if there is some signal, there is definitely a whole lot of noise. But where is the noise in those *Wine Spectator* results? Are their critics superhuman? Are they really tasting blind?

As far as tasting blind is concerned, and before I go any further, let me be clear that the points I'm making in this chapter refer largely to wine magazines: *Wine Spectator*, Robert Parker's *Wine Advocate, Wine Enthusiast*, and so on. There are numerous great wine critics and writers out there—many of whom write for newspapers, or who maintain wine blogs—to whom this critique does not apply. Some critics do taste blind, and many don't use numerical ratings for wines. However, in the modern wine industry, Robert Parker and *Wine Spectator*—perhaps in part because of the mere fact that they do assign 100-point ratings—exert a more powerful influence over the industry, and over price trends, than do the other critics.

So, do the magazine critics taste blind? Well, Robert Parker himself, for one—the father of the US wine-magazine industry and inventor of the 100-point rating scale—doesn't. He freely admits that he sometimes rates wine based on non-blind tasting. This is just one of the axes on which his integrity has been increasingly questioned lately. Wine blogger Tyler Colman, who goes by "Dr. Vino," has undertaken a fascinating series of exposés of Parker and his staff, first (in April 2009) reporting that Parker's right-hand man at the *Wine Advocate*, Jay Miller, had accepted lavish junkets—private plane rides and such—from various coalitions of foreign wine producers.[17]

A couple of years ago, I became similarly curious about the integrity of *Wine Spectator*, whose high scores correlate with high prices just as Parker's do. I undertook an investigation of the magazine's restaurant awards program, the "Wine Spectator Awards of Excellence," which supposedly honors the restaurants with the best wine programs in the world. The magazine also charges restaurants a $250 "entry fee" to participate. I was curious about whether the Awards of Excellence program, which grosses well over $1 million annually for the magazine, represented real expert judgment, or whether it really just functioned as an advertising scheme.

To find out, I decided to apply for an award myself. I created a fictitious Milan restaurant, "Osteria L'Intrepido," whose high-priced "reserve wine list" was composed almost entirely of *Wine Spectator*'s lowest-rated Italian wines from the past couple of decades. These were the wines with ratings in the 60s and 70s—wines deemed undrinkable by *Wine Spectator*'s own critics. And I priced them in the hundreds of euros.

I posted that wine list on a website I created for the imaginary restaurant. I submitted an application for Osteria L'Intrepido along with the $250 fee, jumped through all the requisite hoops, and lo and behold, I won the Award of Excellence, as published in the August 2008 issue of *Wine Spectator*. The only communication I ever received from *Wine Spectator*, at any point, was one voicemail informing me that I'd won the award, and asking if I'd like to purchase an additional $3,000 to $8,000 in advertising in the issue to further publicize my award. The story and materials are still up on my blog at blindtaste.com.[18]

So what happened after the "Awards of Excellence" program was revealed to be a massive million-dollar fraud, an abuse of expert authority, a violation of the public trust for pure financial gain? Not even so much as an apology to their own readers. Interestingly, though, the magazine still makes almost as big a deal about blind wine tasting as I do. James Laube, one of *Wine Spectator*'s senior editors, has gone so far as to write a blog entry about the importance of blind tasting. "*Wine Spectator* has always believed in blind tastings," Laube explains. "We know the region, the vintage and the grape variety, if relevant. But we don't know the producer or the price."[19]

Consider that statement for a moment: the magazine critics are tasting blind, but they know the region, the vintage, and the grape variety. Let's say it's a red wine, the appellation is Hermitage,[20] and the vintage is 2005. The cheapest possible wine in the *Wine Spectator* database that would fit those criteria costs $49. And, to their credit, these tasters certainly know enough about wine to know that Hermitage reds are going to be expensive. In that example, then, they would know the price, or at least the price category, before tasting—which means that they wouldn't really be tasting blind. They'd know that they were tasting expensive wines, and they'd have full frontal exposure to the placebo effect.

At least Laube admits that his staff is only human. "Even the professionals 'miss' a wine now and then," writes Laube, "the same way the refs miss a call. But we believe that if we can eliminate any possibility of bias, we're at least giving you a fair and honest assessment of the wines." Luckily for Laube, it seems that his team of professionals hasn't "missed a call" and accidentally scored a wine under $10 above 91 in at least the past 6,475 tries.

One of the more compelling scenes in the 2004 documentary film *Mondovino* depicts fashion-empire family member and wine producer Salvatore Ferragamo hanging out with James Suckling, the *Wine Spectator* critic who rates Ferragamo's wine for the magazine. If you haven't seen *Mondovino*, it's worth it just to check out this priceless little scene, which could be straight out of Borat: the joke's on Suckling, but he doesn't seem to know it.

Suckling seems to fancy himself a sort of ambassador for Italian wine in the modern era: "Italian wine is the wine of our generation," says Suckling. "Our parents drank French wines, wore Hèrmes, went to Paris. Our generation, we wear Armani, Ferragamo...Prada, and then we drink Italian wines, eat Italian food, and travel to Florence, Rome, Venice." Talking about the 90 he's awarded to Ferragamo's wine, Suckling says: "I was generous, I thought. But he is my landlord." Then the two joke about the idea of renegotiating Suckling's rent for a 95.

None of the evidence in *Mondovino*—or anywhere else—is quite sufficient to prove that there's any actual exchange of influence happening here. Suckling and Ferragamo, of course, are just joking around when they talk about paying for high ratings. And it's not quite impossible—just statistically improbable—that *Wine Spectator* critics are among the only people in the world with perfect palates.

But what kind of message does it send that the magazine continues to accept and publish full-page advertisements for many of the same wines it's reviewing and scoring? And what kind of message does it send to everyday wine drinkers that Suckling—and, by extension, *Wine Spectator*—openly flaunts a buddy-buddy relationship with the producer whose wines he's scoring?

A new *Journal of Wine Economics* paper by Jonathan Reuter is the first to provide concrete evidence that *Wine Spectator* ratings are influenced by advertising. Reuter's model—discussed in greater detail in chapter 8, "New Experimental Results"—found a statistically significant one-point advertising effect in *Wine Spectator* ratings. Although Reuter offered certain alternative explanations for the effect, I find the most obvious explanation to be more likely: that advertising can influence ratings in wine magazines.

It is particularly fitting, I think, that Suckling should be hanging out with a fashion maven, of all people. Because, as I suggest in the next chapter, the wine industry and its magazine critics (not to mention its judges of "excellence" in restaurant wine programs) are looking more like fashionistas every day.

And in the end, corrupt or not corrupt, placebo effects or perfect palates, the problem is the same: magazine critics' results have little in common with the palates of everyday wine drinkers. Why, then, would everyday wine drinkers expect that they'd be any more likely to enjoy a 95-point wine than an 80-point wine? Why, for that matter, should everyday wine drinkers pay any attention at all to those numerical ratings?

# Chapter 4 Dom Pérignon's new clothes

So far we've seen that human beings are pretty suggestible when it comes to wine. The suggestion from some magazine critics, their integrity notwithstanding, is that we should like expensive wine more than cheap wine. We have also seen that when we know a wine is expensive or highly rated, we actually do like it more—our brains' pleasure areas even light up on brain scans. The high prices of prestigious wines have started the engine of the placebo effect, and the magazine critics' endorsement of the price-quality relationship has added fuel. Even if we like it more, there is another component that goes into our choice to spend so much more for expensive wine: the desire to be seen owning and drinking it.

The act of buying, serving, and drinking expensive wine, beyond the mere sensory experience, can provide a way for people to display their wealth, taste, and sophistication to other people—a form of conspicuous consumption. I think of it as an aspirational act: behavior driven by the aspiration to be part of the next higher social class, a token of a more expensive and desirable way of life. As such, conspicuous consumption is actually more associated with the new-money middle class than with the old-money upper class; members of the upper class tend to be less brand-driven, or at least more discreet, with their spending. That's why you see more Champagne consumed in Vegas than in Reims, where it's made.

Of course, extreme conspicuous consumption is the exception to the rule; by no means is every oenophile an aspirational consumer. But there is evidence that the aspirational element is a major part of a wine purchase decision. And whom does the evidence come from? None other than the marketing experts who are telling vintners how to get their wine sold at the chosen price point. Not by changing anything inside the bottle, but unabashedly advising that the change be focused *outside* the bottle.[21] Or, to quote the opening research question in an academic article on the placebo effect in wine, "To which degree should a winery invest in its winemaking practices or in the packaging and promotion of its wines?" Yikes.[22]

We all might have a bit more conspicuous consumption in us than we think. We're in denial, in part because when the placebo effect works, it actually makes the wine taste good, thus making its purchase feel more like a justified exchange at fair market value than an act of conspicuous consumption. Even if you've really paid more for the bottle, label, and marketing than you've paid for the liquid within, it rarely feels that way. And that's how some producers are able to get away with selling premium wines at a markup that would seem insane from any production perspective.

Nowhere is that markup more insane than in the world of sparkling wines. This might happen in part because sparkling wines are probably the most difficult of all wine categories to blind taste and compare; carbon dioxide does a pretty good job of obscuring the differences between them. When you taste sparkling wines, it's a lot easier to detect differences on the nose than on the mouth; in the word of the academics, it's the burst of aerosols from exploding bubbles that makes the drink so unique, as "rising and collapsing bubbles act as a continuous paternoster lift for aromas in every glass of Champagne."[23] But once the bubbles hit your tongue, your ability to sense much beyond sweetness or dryness is significantly stunted.

Try this experiment: taste a couple of sparkling wines just after opening them, and jot down your notes. Then, leave the wines out and open until their fizz disappears. When you taste them again, not only will the wines have changed, they'll also seem much more different from each other than they did initially. Their acidity and oakiness, if any, will become more pronounced, and you'll detect more fruit flavors on the palate.

That's a secret that the premium Champagne producers don't want to let out. Champagne carefully guards its status as a celebratory, special-occasion wine that represents the idea that no expense was spared, whether at a glamorous New Year's Eve party or a wedding. This status makes it a fertile ground for premium markups on unremarkable wines that, in other circumstances, might not be demonstrably better than much cheaper wines.

In the 2007–2008 experiment, our blind tasters sampled more than 350 glasses of 27 sparkling wines, and neither the $150 Dom Pérignon nor the $40 Veuve Clicquot wound up in the top half of those, ratings-wise. And as I mentioned in chapter 1, head to head, 41 of 62 tasters—about two thirds—in the 2007–2008 tastings preferred a $12 Domaine Ste. Michelle Brut from Washington State to the Dom; this year, on a smaller scale, 70% preferred the Ste. Michelle to the Dom, and 85% preferred the Ste. Michelle to the Veuve.

The placebo effect aside, why shouldn't Dom and Veuve—given their perennial popularity with everyday wine drinkers, not just experts—do better, at least, than that?

A peek at Moët Hennessy Louis Vuitton, also known as LVMH, owner of both the Dom Pérignon and Veuve Clicquot brands, offers a clue. Aside from Champagne and those famously imitated handbags, the LVMH portfolio is a roll call of the world's aspirational luxury lifestyle brands: Acqua di Parma, Belvedere and Chopin vodka, Christian Dior perfume and watches, Château d'Yquem wine, Fendi, Givenchy, Guerlain, Kenzo, Krug, Marc Jacobs, Sephora, TAG Heuer, and so on.

The company also runs the consumer branch of De Beers, the diamond empire, and—surprise, surprise—a vast network of duty-free shops at airports around the world. LVMH, which recorded 2009 revenues of €17.1 billion—higher, to give you an idea, than Google's revenues for the same period—is probably the world's most successful practitioner of selling conspicuous consumption. At the end of a year that saw the worldwide economy continue to suffer, LVMH had its best month ever.

But how much is the company actually spending on making Champagne? Well, they don't make that exact information public, but in 2007, LVMH reported that only 35% of revenues went toward the cost of goods, while 43%—that's $11 billion—went to the cost of sales, marketing, and overhead.[24] In contrast,

Constellation Brands, the monster wine conglomerate in the US mass-market wine world, reported in its 2007 annual report that, on the cost side, 58% of revenues went toward the cost of goods, while Constellation spent just 12% of revenues on the cost of sales, marketing, and overhead:[25]

| Company | 2007 revenues | Cost of goods | Sales, marketing, and overhead |
|---------|---------------|---------------|-------------------------------|
| LVMH | $26 billion | $9 billion (35% of revenues) | $11 billion (43% of revenues) |
| Constellation | $6.4 billion | $3.7 billion (58% of revenues) | $768 million (12% of revenues) |

Bernard Arnault, chairman and CEO of LVMH, recently made the point by omission for anyone who cares about what's in the bottle. Boasting of high revenues and profits, he said: "The 2010 first half results, once again, demonstrate the exceptional appeal of our brands as well as the effectiveness of our strategy."[26] Sounds like your standard innocuous corporate statement, right? But when you think about it for a moment, it's interesting that, amidst brand appeal and strategy effectiveness, there isn't a mention of the quality of the goods themselves.

It's starting to look less surprising that the liquid inside Dom Pérignon might not taste so much better than the liquid inside a much cheaper bottle: we're paying our portion of glossy advertisements, corporate sponsorships, armies of top-tier MBAs in fantastic offices, parties at the world's most exclusive nightclubs, and a payroll that includes Tiger Woods, Claudia Schiffer, Catherine Deneuve, André Agassi, Steffi Graf, and Mikhail Gorbachev (who has clearly come a long way from his work leading a communist country). And they advertise that payroll. Why do we fall for it?

Well, flip through LVMH's annual report, and you'll discover that the company seems to have found the consumer-products-industry holy grail: a rare phenomenon known in economics as a Veblen good. Microeconomic theory predicts that the demand for a normal good decreases when the price goes up. But Veblen goods—named for the social theorist Thorstein Veblen, author of *The Theory of the Leisure Class*—are things that people actually want more when the price is raised.

Justin Weinberg, a philosopher at the University of South Carolina, has suggested that expensive wines often function as Veblen goods—that a wine's high price alone can be "sufficient to stimulate a strong interest in consuming it."[27] In the case of premium-priced Champagne, the more it costs, the more impressive it is—even to ourselves. In some cases, the pleasure we're getting from the expensive bottle might even have virtually nothing to do with what's inside, and everything to do with the label, the image, and simply the price we've paid.

That language might sound familiar to the authors of the LVMH annual report, who boasted that "the [Champagne] brand continued its very strong international media presence through the 'Be Fabulous' promotional campaign. ... The Wines and Spirits business group recorded organic revenue growth of 13%, driven by the increase in volumes...and the implementation of a policy to raise prices." The report continues: "the Moët Hennessy distribution network applied the planned price increases, thus strengthening its premium positioning."

*Increase* the price of Champagne to strengthen positioning? It makes sense for LVMH, but it makes no sense for the consumer. In the words of Plassmann and Rangel, authors of the study on the effect of wine's price on reported pleasure, "What happens to the efficiency of competitive markets when firms can influence experienced utility by changing the price of items?"[28]

LVMH seems to know they've got a Veblen good on their hands, and they can barely contain the enthusiasm (within the constraints of sedate Wall Street lingo, anyway) to convey that point to their shareholders. But they also seem to know that they can only continue to pull it off if they keep marketing their wine like a perfume, a diamond ring, a leather bag, or a Swiss watch, which means keeping Woods, Schiffer, and Gorbachev on board, too, and spending billions doing it.

At some point, the annual report moves on to Cognac, un-ironically describing the "major promotional plans" that "enhanced and intensified the dynamic image of the brand," telling of "an advertising campaign...titled Flaunt Your Taste," which "gave Hennessy high visibility and an enhanced image of sophistication."

"Flaunt Your Taste." Veblen couldn't have put it any better had he worked for LVMH.

What saves fashion mavens from the deepest sort of ridicule is that they don't take themselves too seriously. They seem to know how arbitrary their tastemaking is, and understand the absurdity of declaring one dress to be worth $10,000 and another to be worth $50. There's a certain tongue-in-cheek aspect to their attitude; they embrace the ridiculousness of their expert opinions.

As such, to lodge an exposé of the fashion industry's lack of substance would be to attack a straw man. I doubt that anybody who spends $10,000 on a dress is under the delusion that it's 200 times more attractive than something they could get at H&M. Rather, fashionistas seem to revel in the ridiculousness of the expenditure, in the arbitrariness of an of-the-moment anointment. They seem comfortable with the idea that who's wearing something is more important than what's being worn, and are comfortable with the idea that it's probably something that will go out of fashion next year and come back three decades hence. The fashion world is the very definition of self-conscious conspicuous consumption. It is what it is, and it knows what it is.

But wine can be, and should be, something more substantive than that. As Miles Thomas points out in an article on the psychology of wine consumption, "From the Bacchanal to the Sacrament, wine has had a peculiarly sacred place in human history."[29] And since the days of Plato and Aristotle, it has been suggested that ideas more rigorous, scientific, and philosophical can emerge from the enterprise of creating, tasting, and thinking about wine. It was that sentiment that led Alexandre Dumas to famously dub wine the "intellectual part" of the meal.

But when you consider the fact that rigorous blind tasting is still the exception in the world of wine ratings—and the rule is fuzzy, pretentious wine talk and a relentless drive toward proving to the world one's own ability to appreciate best what's most expensive—we wine enthusiasts start to look a lot more like the Champagne-guzzlers in Vegas than like the philosophers in Athens who looked toward wine for meditation, reflection, and self-exploration.

# Chapter 5 So what?

Is there anything really wrong with this whole picture? Some interpreters of the evidence presented in this book have suggested that the placebo effect and conspicuous consumption are forms of consumer welfare that should be welcomed, not questioned. Apologists for the state of things have argued that when you buy a product, you are not just acquiring its physical usefulness; you're also purchasing what economists might call the "social utility" of being associated with the brand. You're buying into a perceived lifestyle, and it makes you happy.

"Conspicuous consumption and waste are an important part of social display," observes the *Economist* in an article about Plassmann and Rangel's work. "Deployed properly, they bring the rewards of status and better mating opportunities. For this to work, though, it helps if the displaying individual really believes that what he is buying is not only more expensive than the alternative, but better, too. Truly enjoying something simply because it is exclusive thus makes evolutionary sense."[30]

Moving on to the practical implications for the business world, the *Economist* article points out that "Rangel's research also has implications for retailers, marketing firms and luxury-goods producers. It suggests that a successful marketing campaign can not only make people more interested in a product, but also, truly, make them enjoy it more."

Although the article does not specifically suggest that this would justify the value to the economy of those marketing campaigns, the implication seems to be there. That is, it wouldn't be much of a stretch to conclude that people's greater actual enjoyment of expensive goods once they know they're expensive justifies, from an economic standpoint, their high buy-in costs—and, by implication, their high marketing expenditures.

The fact that people like prestigious wine, in other words, means that the money that's been spent marketing its prestige has been spent well. It means that consumers benefit from all those good, expensive feelings exactly as they should, and nobody loses in the process. If $150 of pleasure is created by the combination of a marketing campaign and the $150 price tag itself, why should we mind? Can't we just dismiss this as a happy, if irrational, corner of the free market working properly?

Not in my view. When price alone can win over people's palates, winemakers lose their incentive to make wines that people would like if they were blind tasting—wines with intrinsically appealing qualities.

In the case of Champagne, interestingly enough, two French investigators, Olivier Gergaud and Annick Vignes, tried to answer the question of how consumers construct a notion of high quality in their mind, and of what kind of information or quality signals they use in these determinations.[31] Their conclusion was that in the case of a complex good, rankings based on quality signals can be dissonant with those based on taste. When considering only bottles, labels, and prices (that is to say, not tasting the Champagne), people favoured either well-rated (Gosset) or well-known (Veuve Clicquot) brands. Things changed in the subsequent blind tasting. In this situation, people no longer distinguished high ratings, high reputations, or high prices. As the authors concluded, "Our study demonstrates that the most expensive and most heavily advertised products do not systematically coincide with the ones the consumers prefer." This result, discussed further in chapter 8, "New Experimental Results," is in line with other studies showing that very often, people are unable to give values to different Champagnes after tasting, but that this changes when labels are disclosed.

One astonishing result pointed out by the authors is the instability of individual rankings through the experiment: for the most part, one subject's rankings did not match up at all to another's rankings. But when the price was visible, the rankings matched up better, falling into a fairly predictable price-based order. The econometric analysis shows that price remains a major source of information, even among a population of economists. It is a shortcut that we all use, you might say, to make sense of a complex world. But especially in the world of wine, it can be a dangerous shortcut indeed.

In spite of the fascinating new research that has been done in recent years, the neural underpinnings of the price effect are still ill understood. But, from a behavioral standpoint, I hypothesize that the price effect has a lot to do with attention: perhaps we simply pay more attention when we're drinking wine that we're told is expensive. We turn from passive drinkers to active drinkers. We keep the wine in our mouths longer, knowing that with each mouthful, we're swallowing away dollars, not cents. Our mind's eye investigates each of the wine's sensory properties, instead of drinking for simple enjoyment or easy inebriation. For a moment, we give of ourselves, and we get back more. Where we search for complexity, we find it. Where we seek beauty, it arises.

If we did that with every glass of wine we drank—not just the expensive ones—it would enable cheap wines to give us that expensive-wine experience. Not every bottle will do so, of course, but every bottle will have the chance to do so. To accept the premises of this book and pay real attention to every glass you drink is to shift the burden back onto the luxury producers to make a product that actually differentiates itself. Mere attention, perhaps, can set us free.

When consumers pay attention and liberate their palates from the placebo effect, wineries are forced compete to make better-tasting wines, not just better-branded ones, and the bar of quality for the wine industry is raised. Competition on the merits raises the quality of all wines. It encourages producers whose wines give us little—even upon attention and reflection—to offer more. But when wineries compete merely to market their wines more successfully, the consumer loses, because more resources go toward marketing, and fewer toward winemaking. A great winemaker is your friend, but one that substitutes marketing for winemaking is the enemy of the wine consumer. And a company that spends as much (or more) money on marketing as it does on research, development, and production—a company like LVMH—is delivering poor value to consumers. When we pay their premiums and fund their advertising campaigns, we are literally *paying* them to tell us that *we* like their product.

Marketing wasn't always about appealing to our social or emotional insecurities, and it wasn't always a waste of resources. Look at any pre-World War II magazine, and you'll see pages full of advertisements that actually discussed the substantive advantages of their products. For instance, a pair of shoes or a shirt would be advertised as having more durable soles or better fabric. That sort of advertising served an informational purpose: it informed the consumer about the product's availability and about the real differences between that product and others. It cast the product onto the consumer's radar screen, and the dissemination of that information helped the market function fluidly.

That's not what's going on when you see a wine associated with a scantily clad woman, a celebrity, or a kangaroo, or branded with a name like "Mommy's Time Out," "Four Emus," "Little Black Dress," or "Old Fart." What do these names have to do with wine? The information dissemination has been replaced by brands elbowing for emotional space in consumers' minds. Effective modern wine marketing is rarely about communicating the way the wine tastes or smells; it's more about communicating a lifestyle. It's about preying on our social needs—the same needs that drive our tendency toward conspicuous consumption—rather than our sensory ones.

In economic terms, the marketing of consumer products in the modern world is a zero-sum game. Every time a consumer chooses one sparkling wine over another based on marketing, and not on the results of blind tastings, the one company wins and another loses. But the money that both have spent competing on lifestyle marketing is wasted. For every winner, there's a loser. And since the consumer ultimately pays for the marketing, whoever wins, the consumer always loses.

The emergence of emotional marketing, and the accompanying replacement of true consumer choice with an opaque network of intermediaries and social forces, is hardly limited to the wine industry. Take cars, for instance. In the last gasps of the gilded age, even as General Motors was beginning to crumble, Cadillac turned into a fascinating study in modern marketing: on the verge of obsolescence, the company managed to reposition its image completely, from Eldorado to Escalade, turning itself from the canonical conspicuous-consumption emblem of Morty Seinfeld's generation into the canonical conspicuous-consumption emblem of Jay-Z's generation.

The still-not-quite-dead Cadillac brand launched a new motto, which you can still find scrawled across many of its highway billboard ads. It is simply this: "Life, liberty, and the pursuit."

Veblen would love it: "of happiness" has been cut from a phrase that has, for generations, been understood to embody the essence of the American spirit. Happiness, it seems, is no longer the point. It's just "the pursuit."

The pursuit of what?

# Fearless Critic restaurant guides from the editorial team behind *The Wine Trials*

Now online and at bookstores nationwide

# **Chapter 6** Critics and critiques

Blind tasting is not a one-sided issue. There has been some sophisticated discussion about its pros and cons. The *New York Times* wine writer Eric Asimov, in an interesting series of articles, has argued that blind tasting is insufficient as a way to judge wine. In his first such article, which came out before the first edition of this book, Asimov argues that "blind tastings eliminate knowledge and context that can be significant in judging a wine...I feel it's a little like judging a book by reading one chapter or one page."[32] Insisting on blind tasting—continues Asimov in his second post on the subject—prevents you from understanding the wine you're judging: "It's almost an anti-intellectual position. Obviously what's in the glass matters. But I think the more knowledge you can bring to a wine, the better your understanding of that wine will be."[33]

Asimov's part in this debate over the merits of blind tasting intensified after he responded on his blog to a *Newsweek* article about this book that came out in advance of its publication, and then again after having read the galleys. His writing on the subject culminated in a print article in the *Times*, which, along with the blog posts and lively exchange of reader comments, would make good reading for anyone interested in this book.[34, 35]

When positions become polarized, of course, the subtlety of each side's thought is muted, and straw men show up. I doubt, for instance, that Asimov really takes me to be arguing that wine writers shouldn't discuss the story behind a wine, that they shouldn't mention the pudding stones of Châteauneuf-du-Pape or the eccentricities of Josko Gravner and his amphorae. In fact, we discuss just those sorts of stories in the second half of this book, where we review wines. Our descriptions do not rely solely on blind tasting notes. Without a doubt, a lot of the fun of wine is in all the stuff that's not in the glass.

Indeed, to drink a wine blind with dinner, thus neutralizing all the sensory/emotional value we get from our brain's processing of the extrinsic facts about a wine—the same value that's demonstrated by the experiments cited in this book—would be the greatest folly of all. The intellectual enterprise of wine appreciation that Dumas described would be incomplete without knowing what wine one is thinking or talking about. In fact, if the wine is expensive, telling everyone how much it cost you—though gauche—might even help your guests enjoy it more.

The more interesting point that Asimov makes is about the artificiality of any blind-tasting experiment—first and foremost, about the fact that wine is meant to be drunk with food, and that it is inherently problematic to judge it in isolation. "I personally think wine is experienced in a different way," he writes, "when it's consumed with a meal over time, and that's one reason why, in this blog, I do not write about wines that I've only sipped in tastings." Asimov rails against "the mass-tasting environment," arguing that "it's a completely unnatural way to taste and to judge wine. Rather than drink wine in a natural environment with food, wines are pitted against each other, sipped and spit, one after another."

Most wine is better and more complex with food; there's no doubt about that. There's a fair argument to be made that when your goal is to maximize your sheer pleasure from wine, you should only drink it with food. Even terrible wine can taste good with the right food.

But to seriously evaluate wine together with food is to make a similar mistake as evaluating it non-blind: it confounds the results of an already unscientific process—the subjective sensory evaluation of wine—with dozens of other even less predictable variables.

It is true that information about your experience of a wine in the absence of food, or in a sequence of other wines, will not be perfectly relevant to a reader's future experience of that same wine over a relaxing meal. But information about how the wine's fruit character and tannins reacted with your next-door neighbor's demi-glace might well be even less relevant.

The more important problem with Asimov's general critique, though, is that to dismiss blind tasting as superficial is to sidestep the troubling realities of the current marketplace that blind tasting aims to address. The central problem in the wine world is not that too many wine critics aren't pairing wine with food, or that wine companies are turning out too many bottles.

The central problem is that wine pricing is almost completely arbitrary—that the price of wine does not significantly correlate to the pleasure it brings, even to experts.

It's that Robert Parker, *Wine Spectator*, and others with economic power in the industry are propping up the myth that price and pleasure do correlate strongly, that it really is possible that not one of 6,475 wines under $10 would score above 91. It's that generations of consumers are now growing up taking that myth as fact, and drinking and buying wine in a way that conforms to the myth.

Some of the biggest victims of this state of affairs are the very "artisanal, natural or hand-crafted categories" that Asimov so admires. Their livelihoods hang in the balance. Most of them learn, often through trial and error, that to get a truly high rating in (or even to be acknowledged by) most wine magazines, your wine must first be expensive; and to justify charging that much, you must make it in a certain style and hire a certain consultant; and before you know it, you've made not the wine you wanted to make, but rather the wine the magazine told you to make.

Of all the winemakers with whom I've spoken about this set of issues, I can't think of one that was comfortable with the power held by, or the reliability of, the institutions that assign point scores to wine. If there is a single issue that most irks good, honest wine producers, it's the grip held on them by this network of corrupt-at-worst, highly-suggestible-at-best 100-point tastemakers; these tastemakers' junketeering; and their blind reverence for the super-premium Screaming Eagle/Sassicaia/Pétrus/Vega Sicilia/Penfolds Grange hierarchy. Producers who are simply trying to make good wine and sell it at a fair price complain about this situation even more than they complain about the unpredictability of the weather.

There is no circumstance in which it is justifiable for one person—yes, Robert M. Parker, Jr.—to unilaterally affect the prices of *en primeur* Bordeaux wines, as shown in a clever study in the *The Economic Journal* by Lecocq, Visser, and their colleague Héda Hadj Ali.[36] Perhaps some form of ratings—or at least recommendations—must exist, with or without food pairings. But it's inappropriate for a magazine's tasters—just before assigning an evaluative score that is likely to have a major impact on the wine's price, on its availability to everyday wine drinkers, and on the producer's financial well-being—to be told that the wine they're about to taste is a 2005 Pomerol, or (on the other end of the spectrum) a Merlot from Baja California.

In those cases, the placebo effect—which, as Brochet and Weil have shown, applies to experts just as it does to everyday wine drinkers—colors the evaluation: good wines from humble or stigmatized regions are penalized; average wines from famous, expensive regions are rewarded; and the chronic overrating and overpricing of prestige wines is perpetuated.

This is the vicious cycle of non-blind rating that has poisoned the modern wine industry. It is the cycle that has driven the release price of a good vintage of Pétrus to $5,000 per bottle, and it is the cycle that maintains the price of Dom Pérignon at $150. Everybody inside or outside the industry who knows better should speak out against the poisonous myth spread by so much of the wine establishment that while not every expensive wine must be great, every great wine must be expensive.

The aim of *The Wine Trials 2011*—aside from seeking out good, widely available values under $15—is to question the institutional structures that govern the industry, to encourage people to learn their own palates through the exercise of tasting blind instead of trusting the numerical scores that Parker and the magazines assign. It is the economic power of these institutional structures that damages not only the wallet of the everyday consumer, but also the chances for a small, interesting, good-value producer—even one that makes wine costing more than $15—to succeed on the store shelf or on the restaurant wine list.

Anyone who seeks to defend those producers' prospects for success should join in and speak out against the pay-to-play schemes at the wine magazines and other publications whose main business is selling ads to the very wineries whose products they evaluate. Their incentives are twisted from the start, and there is enormous anecdotal evidence that even if an ad won't guarantee you a high rating, it will increase the chances that your wine will at least be reviewed in the publication—which, for smaller producers, is often the tougher battle. It is time for people who care about wine to hold the irresponsible critics accountable, because their market manipulations currently threaten the fabric of the industry.

As things stand, our society of wine drinkers—and consumers of other goods—rides on the placebo effect more than most people are willing to admit. My hope is that once you've begun tasting blind, the placebo effect will fade in favor of something better: the pleasure of enjoying a good wine at a good price—and a wine that you know is good, however little you might have paid.

Once you're choosing wine purely on its merits, you've taken away the power of lifestyle marketing, and you've enhanced your ability to find pleasure in an inexpensive bottle—and, for that matter, in an expensive one, too. You've become a real consumer.

Although glossy magazines might have you believe otherwise, the choice to buy a wine—or to buy anything else—on the reputation of a brand alone is a sacrifice of your individuality, not an expression of it. America is the country that spread free-market capitalism around the world, yet by accepting what we're told products are worth instead of determining their value for ourselves, we're turning our version of capitalism into something else. We're withdrawing the consumer's power to shape the demand curve that is meant to keep the market at equilibrium. In the swordfight of supply and demand, we're laying down our weapons and bowing before the supply curve, letting producers unilaterally tell us what we want—and at what price. That's not a healthy free market. That's LVMH's Five-Year Plan.

To be a skeptical consumer—to look past the tastemakers and magazines, to experience the liquid and judge wine on its pure underlying merits, and to learn about the wine while you're at it— is to flex the fingers of capitalism's invisible hand, to push the system to work the way that it is supposed to work.

But to surrender, instead, to the siren song of marketing and price signals—to buy what you're told to buy, or to assume that expensive means good—is to withdraw your own brain from free participation in our own market economy. It is not just self-destructive. It is, to me, un-American.

# Chapter 7 The culture war

> No man also having drunk old wine
> straightway desireth new: for he saith,
> The old is better.
> *–King James Bible,* Luke 5:39

What is the purpose of wine? Is it meant to be served before dinner, with dinner, or with dessert? Is it meant to be drunk in your living room, on the beach, or at a world-class restaurant? The answer, of course, is all of the above, and the answers to what wine should taste like are different in each of these situations.

Beyond that, though, one of the central themes of this book has been that even when people are in controlled blind-tasting settings—even when they are confronted with the exact same wines as each other, in the exact same situations—there is often not much agreement between them over which wines are best.

There are the New World wine lovers and the Old World wine lovers; there are the fruit-and-oak lovers and the earth-and-mineral lovers; and there is everything in between. There are people who love Australian Shiraz with sushi on the beach, and people who will drink Sancerre in front of the fireplace on a cold winter's night. I have seen a group of Hong Kong businessmen mix 1970

Château Latour with Coca-Cola before drinking it. People's preferences in wine vary wildly, even within the ranks of those that have gone through extensive training—not to mention the difference between consumers with and without training.

When you figure in genetic differences, differences in upbringing, differences in understanding about what purpose wine is supposed to serve, and differences in mood or body chemistry on a given day or at a given moment, blind tasting data become so noisy that one needs to collect thousands of data points to get any statistically significant results at all. This is true even when the tasters are all experienced wine professionals. "Variation in judgment, even among experts," write Amerine and Roessler, "is why we reject single-judge evaluations."

Yet amidst this culture war, the world of wine criticism is coming to be dominated by exactly those types of single-judge evaluations. Amidst all this instability and dissent in the wine world, there is one relatively sure thing: that as the global industry modernizes its equipment and winemaking style, it is converging on one stylistic direction, one basic taste profile. Many expensive wines seem to have mastered that style; inexpensive wines are emulating it everywhere; and the style is catching on all around the world, even in traditionally non-wine-drinking countries.

The style is specific, it's easily identifiable, and it is more commonly found in wines made by modern producers from the New World (e.g. the United States and Australia) than wines made by traditional producers from the Old World (e.g. France, Spain, Portugal, and Italy), although this is rapidly changing.[37] The single most recognizable aspect of the style is that it plays to the world's sweet tooth.

Proponents of the modern New World style tend to describe it with words like jammy, fruit-forward, big, full-bodied, and concentrated. Opponents complain that New World methods create similar wines, regardless of the region, resulting in a convergence of the world's wine styles and a loss of diversity.

Then there is the Old World style, whose proponents like to talk about it as balanced, elegant, sometimes austere, and, at its best, faithfully representative of a particular terroir (the unique characteristics of a region's geography, climate, soil, and so on). Old World wine often takes more time to mature than does New World wine.

You may fall upon either side of the divide; there's certainly no shame in liking concentrated New World fruit, or in disliking Old World acidity, dustiness, and minerality. What's hard to debate, though, is that the New World style is currently winning the race by a landslide. The runaway success of the Australian wine brand Yellow Tail—whose Chardonnay and Shiraz are now the world's two best-selling wines, each selling more than 20 million bottles per year—is evidence enough of that, as is the fact that even famous, centuries-old Old World wines, including first-growth Bordeaux, are slowly converting to the New World style.

One culprit for this is the convergence of academic studies and marketing forces. In one such study recently published (and also discussed in chapter 8, "New Experimental Results")—a study that, alas, seems commissioned by those very forces of marketing—researchers at the Australian Wine Institute sought to determine what sensory attributes most drive consumer and expert acceptance for Cabernet Sauvignon and Shiraz wines.[38] The winemakers' quality scores had little relationship with consumer response, and were based on a different set of sensory attributes. So far, so good. But having identified the properties of red wine that consumers prefer the authors go on to suggest that winemakers could maximize certain sensory properties, "allowing producers to better meet consumers' preferences." This is a dangerous path toward a bland convergence. It amounts to saying: if the prevailing taste is dumb, dumb down your wine. The customer always knows best.

It has become quite common in food and wine circles to blame (or thank, depending on your perspective) Robert Parker for all of this. The influence of the world's most famous wine critic is powerful indeed. But, as has been discussed above, not everybody likes Parker's palate, and it's also fashionable in certain circles (especially the restaurant industry) to hate Parker and his "big, dumb wines." It's too easy, though, and quite misleading, to blame Parker for the current state of affairs in the wine world. As I write in a 2010 review of his new guide to wines under $25 in the *Journal of Wine Economics*, he is more of a rhetorician than a critic in the classic sense:[39]

> [Parker's] longstanding success does not derive from his ability...to pick out blackberry or tobacco from a wine's

bouquet...or from any other of kind consumer advocacy. It comes, rather, from Parker's talent for escapism, from his confident use of superlatives to capture the sensory imagination.

For most readers, flipping through an issue of *Wine Advocate* and reading about 100-point wines is like flipping through an issue of *Motor Trend*...imagining yourself behind the wheel of a Lamborghini recreates the seventh-grade psyche of perfect possibility that is still buried somewhere in your weary folds of cortical memory. Teenagers feel immortal, people always say. They think the finish really lasts forever.

It is the mix of idolatry and attainability that make Parker's prose so compelling: these wines that win 100 points are described as Platonic forms, yet they're also physical objects with real molecular structures; they're liquids that can, at least in theory, come into contact with your mouth...it's the ontology that matters: the idea that some wines really do win 100, that it is concretely possible to taste perfection, is irresistible.

The very thing that invalidates Parker's writing as nonfiction is what redeems it as fiction: his topic isn't wine. It's human contact with the divine. Many...that have become increasingly disgusted with so-called "Parkerization"...would paint the celebrated critic as a power-hungry dictator with designs on reshaping the wine world just to please his palate and fortify his wealth. But to adopt that view is to misunderstand the fundamental human mechanics of Parker's vast appeal. Winemakers may feel obliged to please him, but consumers are under no obligation to follow him. If you want to understand Parker, look in the mirror.

Robert Parker is no dictator. He is a storyteller. The magnetism of his prose is that of J.K. Rowling's, too: you're first presented with a set of familiar facts and situations, and then, slowly, you're seduced into suspending reason and believing in the perfectly impossible. Escape into a Parker review, and for a few sentences, there you are, back in junior high, the great critic's palate—and yours, too—cured of its nagging mortality. In this counterfactual place, there is no perceptual bias, just perception. There is no confidence interval, just confidence. Parker's 100-point wine is Gatsby's green light, the orgiastic ghost of taste's future, the tongue a sudden lattice of infinite resolution, the nose a sudden instrument of preternatural whiff.

All of this said, it is indisputable that the Parkerized style of wine is appealing to an increasing percentage of wine drinkers, and the reasons for this are probably more related to our collective upbringing than to anything else. Just as your taste and smell experience can change at a moment's notice when you think you're drinking an expensive wine, your experience can change over time as you acquire preferences for new or different tastes and smells; in psychology and neuroscience, this phenomenon is known as "perceptual learning." Most of us have experienced some version of it as we've grown up. Maybe you didn't like mushrooms or blue cheese when you were a little kid, for instance—and maybe you didn't like wine at all the first time you tried it. (You presumably do now, if you've read this far.)

One thing that kids almost universally like is sugar, and our culture has become uniquely indulgent of that taste. People make a big deal about how American children are growing up on fast food, but at least fast food, for the most part, tastes good. However unhealthy a McDonald's Quarter Pounder with Cheese is, and however suspect the provenance of its ingredients, the burger is well seasoned and has a reasonable balance of tastes and textures. What's totally out of balance, though, is the flavor profile of soft drinks. All health concerns aside, sugar is the silent killer of our nation's palate.

Levels of sugar tolerance vary between people. Domenic and Arnold Cicchetti, in a 2009 study published in the *International Journal of Wine Research*, find that "the recognition threshold level for sugar is between 0.5% and 2.5%, the average taster recognition is only 1%. Consequently, there may be considerable variability in the perception of sugar between any two tasters. What one taster may detect as sweet may seem dry to another, despite the fact that they taste the same wine."[40]

Children are building up an incredibly early taste for sweet things, and in terms of gustatory tolerance, artificial sweeteners are just as bad as sugar. That sweetness has started to dominate the taste of foods whose traditional recipes don't even call for sugar, like salad dressings, mustards, and pasta sauces.

As a result, when many people start drinking wine as adults, they don't even perceive the likes of Yellow Tail as sweet. Wine industry consultant Jon Fredrikson, in an interview with the *New York Times*, has called Yellow Tail "the perfect wine for a public grown up on soft drinks."[41]

Perhaps, then, it shouldn't be surprising that Robert Parker has called the Yellow Tail wines "surprisingly well-made": he, too, grew up on soft drinks. According to Elin McCoy, his biographer, Parker hadn't had a single glass of dry wine until he was 20 years old, on his first trip to France: "Since Coca-Cola was so expensive, a dollar for a tiny bottle, Pat [his girlfriend] insisted he try un verre de vin, the first dry wine Parker had ever tasted."[42]

In other words, the culprit for the style convergence might not be Parker himself, or his followers themselves; it might be the producers' tendency to do whatever will not challenge the public, and it might be the taste for sugar that he—and they—all acquired in childhood, a taste that an increasing percentage of the world's children are also now acquiring. Certainly Parker's rise can be attributed in part to his charisma, his business acumen, his consistent palate, his writing style, and many other factors—but it also might be attributed in part to the fact that people who grew up with a sweet tooth feel vindicated by Parker's palate.

As wine continues to spread to vast swaths of the world whose populations have scarcely encountered it outside of elite hotels—China, Africa, Southeast Asia, India—the natural first tendency amongst new drinkers is the child's instinct: to go for what's sweet, or at least what's very fruity. There is no shame in this, but it is steering the marketplace.

And we see the same thing happening in the swaths of our own country that aren't as steeped in wine tradition—the rural Midwest, the deep South. Could it be that the Parkerization of the world's wine industry owes less to Parker himself, and more to the expansion of the economic pie that free trade and globalization have enabled? Should we call the super-concentrated, super-fruity, sometimes slightly sweet New World style not "Parkerized," but rather "globalized"?


Whether or not you find the globalized style pleasant on a sensory level, a more fundamental problem is that it's a style of wine that's not created by nature, but rather by aggressive intervention with techniques like aging wine in new oak barrels for extended periods of time. What's even more bothersome, though, is the fact that, driven by the ratings of Parker and his progeny, the worlds of cheap and expensive wines all over the world seem to be converging on a single taste profile. As globalized wine is being introduced even to Rioja, the traditional style that has produced unique local wines in those regions is being replaced with one common "international" style that's geared toward getting high scores from magazine critics like Parker and *Wine Spectator*. And we've seen in the previous chapter how much those high scores matter.

As the world's wines grow more similar to each other with each successive vintage, the incredible diversity of the world's wine regions is being lost, and—perhaps due to undue deference to the magazine critics' ratings—the world's high-end wine consumers are supporting the trend with their wallets.

Whatever style of wine you think you like, you owe it to yourself, and to the wine world, to test that assumption scientifically. Either way, it's important that you make sure you agree with the magazine critics, at least, before jumping onto the New World bandwagon.

Recent research on Italian wines delivered the bad news on this topic—and the good news as well. An analysis of consumer response to Veneto DOC wines, discussed in chapter 8 ("New Experimental Research"), showed that brand reputation is a major intrinsic determinant of consumer choice—but the greater the knowledge, the lesser the influence of brand reputation on the consumer.[43]

Maybe for you, a bottle of Screaming Eagle really is worth the $5,000 that it commands. Either way, once you've decided for yourself—firsthand and blind, with only your palate in charge—whether or not the Emperor is dressed, your brain's curious habit of making things taste like you expect them to taste—of making expensive things taste better, and of making cheap things taste worse—might lessen, too.

That's the funny thing about our brains, and about expectations. If this book makes you skeptical of high price tags, just reading it could change the taste of expensive wine for you. What will change your experience even more, though, is blind tasting yourself. By questioning wine prices, you will become less of a slave to expectations and more of a student of your own palate. Invoking only the simple, everyday miracle of the scientific method, you will have turned a placebo into wine.

# Chapter 8 New experimental results

At its core, this blind tasting manifesto is built around the contributions of science to the question of how we understand the perception and enjoyment of wine. Thankfully, more and more researchers are contributing valuable insights to this understanding, and a lot of what was previously left to the realm of anecdotal evidence has become mainstream academic research.

In the year that has passed since the release of our last edition, *The Wine Trials 2010*, new scientific studies have continued to shape the nuances of our views on wine perception while also pointing the way toward future avenues of research. At the risk of sounding self-congratulatory, we believe that many of these new results have confirmed many of the views that we have set forth since first edition of *The Wine Trials*. At the same time, this new research has continued to shape the nuances of these arguments and to guide the direction of future research.

Generally speaking, two main lines of inquiry have emerged. One covers roughly the question of what goes into the pleasure we get from a wine: is it a placebo effect? Is it terroir? Is it marketing? The other area of focus concerns the confidence that ought to be placed in expert judgments, which dramatically affect consumption decisions. These decisions, in turn, affect winemaker's choices of what to produce and how to position it to experts, and ultimately play a huge role in the composition of wine shelves across America. Needless to say, they deserve a lot of attention.

The discussions of expert opinion in the first two editions of *The Wine Trials* have focused largely on the problem that many sources of so-called expertise in wine—magazines, individual critics, wine fair judges, and so on—are often poisoned by bias: some critics taste completely non-blind, while others taste without knowing the producer's name but knowing information that still creates bias, like a wine's appellation, grape varieties, or price, which can present as an even bigger problem insofar as readers are misled to fancy the "blind." Still others have obvious conflicts of interest: they accept PR junkets from industry lobbyists, and thus have an interest in rating the products they're promoting higher so as to be invited on the next junket; or they sell ads to the wineries being evaluated, for instance, and thus have an interest in satisfying their customers.

One of the most interesting scientific results of 2009 in the world of wine expertise and bias was a study by researcher Jonathan Reuter, published as an article in the *Journal of Wine Economics*, which looked at that last topic: the influence of advertising revenue on the ratings in wine magazines. Does advertising in *Wine Spectator*, Reuter asked, get you a higher score? It's a difficult effect to measure, in large part because of the potential for a self-selection effect: that is, if advertisers score higher, it could just mean that better wineries tend to advertise more, not that the magazine is biased toward advertisers. Reuter got around this problem by bringing in a set of ratings data from another publication, *Wine Advocate*, that doesn't sell ads to wineries, and looking at the question of whether wines that advertised in *Wine Spectator* tended to perform comparatively better (in that magazine when compared with their performance in *Wine Advocate*: in other words, whether advertising in *Wine Spectator* was a positive predictive factor in the Wine Spectator-Wine Advocate score difference. The effect found by Reuter was small, but it was positive and statistically significant: his model predicts that a *Wine Spectator* advertiser will score, on average, one point higher than a non-advertiser.

*Wine Spectator* Executive Editor Thomas Matthews responded as follows: "At *Wine Spectator*, every review of a newly-released wine is the result of a blind tasting, where neither producer nor price is known by the taster. This approach gives every wine a fair and equal chance to show its best, and guarantees that no bias can influence the scores."[44]

Interestingly, in the conclusions to his paper, Reuter retreats to the position that seems to comport with Matthews': he "finds little consistent evidence of bias...at worst, the tests for biased ratings suggest that *Wine Spectator* rates wines from advertisers almost one point higher than wines from non-advertisers. However, selective retastings can explain at most half of this bias and then only within the set of U.S. wines rated by both *Wine Spectator* and *Wine Advocate*. Given *Wine Spectator*'s claim that it rates wines blind, the remaining difference in ratings may simply reflect consistent differences in how the two publications rate quality, which leads to predictable differences in advertising. This interpretation is consistent with the fact that tests for biased awards provide no additional evidence of bias. Therefore, despite the fact that *Wine Spectator* is dependent on advertising revenue, the long-run value of producing credible reviews appears to minimize bias."[45]

As I write in my blog, Blind Taste, I think this conclusion is softer than it need be: "Even if selective retastings explain only half of the one-point bias, that's still pretty damning; it means that if you advertise in *Wine Spectator*, you might well get the benefit of a selective retasting that gets you, on average, an additional half-point. Translation: advertising influences ratings. With respect to the other half-point, if there are indeed 'consistent differences in how the two publications rate quality, which leads to predictable differences in advertising,' then you should try leafing through a copy of *Wine Spectator* and seeing if you'd trust critics who favor the types of wines that tend to advertise in the magazine. I think the roster of advertisers speaks for itself."[46]

And lest you think that a one-point difference seems small, consider the distribution of ratings in these magazines: they're crammed into a small subset of the theoretical 100-point range. The *Wine Spectator* scores, for instance, have a mean of about 85.4 and a standard deviation of just 4.7, meaning that two-thirds of ratings are crammed into the 9-point range from 81 to 90, which makes a one-point bump seem pretty significant—it's more than 10% of that range.

In particular, a bump from 89 to 90 points can have a huge effect on a wine's price and prospects for success in the marketplace. Some preliminary research has observed that there's a bump in the wine-ratings bell curve at 90—that is, that more wines score exactly 90 points than would be predicted by the normal distribution. That effect could come from advertising bias, or it could come from a cognitive bias on the part of critics, who see the number as a threshold. Either way, the 89–90 difference is proof that even a one-point bump can have a big impact. Either a tasting is blind or it isn't, and if advertising can buy you that bump, then the critics are for sale.

Not that this doesn't make sense from their business perspective. In his discussion, Reuter considers the "profit maximization problem for a publication that derives revenue from both advertisers and subscribers." Make the reviews too biased, in other words, and you lose subscribers (and in turn ad dollars that are tied to circulation figures). Make the reviews biased below a certain threshold, and you get away with the extra dollars without an offset in terms of dearly departed former subscribers. It would seem that the one-point upward discrepancy—which can earn a winery a significant premium—might just have hit that sweet spot for *Wine Spectator* between maximizing its interests and minimizing the negative effect on its readership, even without any purposefulness on anyone's part. The advertisers are happy, the magazine gets the ad revenue and keeps the subscriptions, and the readership is left holding the bag of corruption and undue influence.

Putting aside non-blind tasting bias and advertising bias, there is another, less-discussed problem with wine expert ratings that has been increasingly bubbling to the top of the wine economics world—and it's a problem that exists even in perfectly controlled blind tasting labs. The problem is the cognitive limitations of wine experts and judges, and more specifically, their inability to rate and rank wines consistently. In particular, when people taste the same wine twice, they often assign wildly different scores to the two experiences. In the large-scale blind tasting experiment we ran whose results were published as the academic paper "Do More Expensive Wines Taste Better?,"[47] one of the scientific building blocks of *The Wine Trials*, we looked at experts' and non-experts' consistency when secretly serving the same wine twice within one flight, and we found that expert tasters didn't do any better than non-experts at ranking the wines similarly.

Applying a much more complex version of this type of test to California state wine fairs, statistics scholar and California winemaker Robert Hodgson has produced the most sophisticated (and disconcerting) analysis ever conducted on the reliability (or, better put, lack thereof) of wine experts in blind tasting situations, much of which has been developed or published in the year since *The Wine Trials 2010* was released. In Chapter 3, we discuss some of Hodgson's latest findings on wine fair medals, whose distribution, he argues, looks dismally evocative of the so-called "binomial distribution" that one would expect to see if the medals were assigned with utter randomness: "winning gold medals," he writes, "may be more a matter of chance than a predictor of quality."[48]

Australian researchers Richard Gawel and Peter W. Godden, meanwhile, tracked wine evaluations by experienced wine judges, looking at the scores assigned by the judges to duplicate presentations of the same wines. Gawel and Godden looked at wine quality scores issued by 571 experienced wine tasters over a 15-year period, focusing on calculating the pooled variation in repeat scores and assessing the ability of the tasters to evaluate wine quality with consistency in blind tastings. While they suggest that tasters showed consistency overall (stopping short of Hodgson's binomial distribution argument), their individual abilities varied considerably (confirming that result in Hodgson's work). Interestingly, the authors also noted that the ability of a taster to consistently score red wines was a poor predictor of his or her consistency in scoring white wines, and vice versa.[49]

Hodgson, working again with data from California state wine competitions, arrived at results that were similar but even more damning. Looking at scores by judges who participated in more than one competition, he found that only about 10% of judges were "consistently consistent"—that is, consistently assigned point scores corresponding to the same medal range to the exact same wine when tasted more than once. The rest of the judges did less well than that, and many were all over the board when tasting the same wine multiple times, for example assigning it a gold medal when tasting it one time, and no medal at all when tasting it a different time. Using a psychometric methodology known as a

Cohen kappa coefficient, which gives a statistical basis to pronounce someone an expert (derived from the variance of the scores they assign to the same wine across multiple tastings), Hodgson found that fewer than 30% of the judges reviewed would qualify.[50, 52]

Coming back to the factors that influence, in myriad ways, the judgment of everyday consumers—a prolific area for a wide variety of inquiries—a few particular studies of note have come out since *Wine Trials 2010*. One of them, by Italian researchers Fiego Begalli, Lara Agnoli, and Stefano Codurri, confirms that brand reputation is a major intrinsic determinant of consumer choice in the DOC region of Veneto, and, more interestingly, that throughout the decision process, consumers are conscious of being influenced by brand marketing—yet are still affected by it. On the positive—and promising—side, the study shows that the greater the knowledge about the intrinsic merits of the good, the lesser the influence of brand reputation on the consumer.[52]

The positive role played by consumer knowledge is also stressed in a recent, but slightly older, French study on Champagne preferences by the excellent Olivier Gergaud and Annick Vignes. Subjects were asked to rank four bottles of Champagne at different times: first, when able to see the bottles but without tasting and without knowledge of prices; second, with information on the bottles and their prices; and in the third and fourth experiments, while blind tasting the same wines in different order (without knowing they were the same). The authors of the study reach two interesting conclusions: first, that well-known brands are significantly better ranked than little-known brands when consumers see the bottles but do not taste the product, but second, significantly, that well-known brands and little-known brands are equally ranked when they are tasted blind and their prior beliefs about quality no longer have a role in the evaluation process. Perhaps promisingly, the research suggests that when consumers receive information signals about Champagne, their preferences depend on their cognitive capacity to understand the information, but when tasting blind, their preferences depend on their levels of oenological knowledge and their actual taste preferences. In other words, given the inconsistency in judgments by each subject, the authors conclude that better information helps rational consumers to discover their preferred product.[53]

In a somewhat different context, Luiz de Mello and Ricardo Pires recently ran an experiment that didn't even need to expose consumers to actual wine. They looked at how consumers (and especially occasional drinkers) infer quality when confronted with labels that do not conform to conventional compositional patterns of colors and shapes. Certain color-shape combinations were taken by consumers as relevant data on which to base a conclusion as to the quality of the bottle's content, while others weren't. While none of this comes as shocking news, it's another reminder of the power of the critter, and just how many potential influences a savvy consumer must keep at bay.[54]

Back inside the bottle, a 2010 study from Australia looked at the discrepancy in assessments of wine quality by everyday consumers on the one hand and expert winemakers on the other. Both groups were asked to blind taste several Australian Shiraz and Cabernet Sauvignon wines, in an attempt to assess how winemakers' judgments of quality might relate to consumer preference. The study found that the winemakers' quality scores relied on an entirely different set of sensory attributes from those of the consumers. As a result, they had little relationship with consumer response to a wine's quality. Winemakers favored higher hotness, astringency, and fruit and oak flavour, in stark contrast to the consumer preference for less imposing wines. Interestingly, the wines that scored highest in the winemaker assessment were generally the more expensive wines.[55] Unfortunately, the conclusion of this study—which seems to have become a stain on many such endeavors—is couched as a supply-side prescription: "This study identifies sensory properties of red wines which could be maximized as well as those which should be reduced, allowing producers to better meet consumers' preferences." Why should the evidence from this study be turned into a marketing directive advising winemakers to make what are, to them, inferior wines? If the consumer always already knows best, then how is he to learn?

A study on the role of emotions in wine consumption in Portugal similarly turns quickly into ammunition for the producers and peddlers. Drawing conclusions on the emotions that wine elicits, the authors of the study, Ramo Barrena and Mercedes Sanchez, suggest that "If they are to improve their strategic positioning in the marketplace...it is of vital importance for producers to identify and understand how consumers respond to relevant aspects of their own personalities through the products they buy and consume."[56] Or, to quote the incriminating research question in an earlier study on the placebo effect in wine, "to which degree should a winery invest in its winemaking practices or in the packaging and promotion of its wines?"[57]

Yikes. For all our celebration of research into wine perception, that is, we must recognize a more pernicious angle in some research projects. In the hands of marketers and sellers—many of whom, indeed, finance these studies—the usefulness of the information can be flipped on its head and deployed in full force to influence consumer decisions based on anything but the intrinsic merits of a wine.

Research in all these fields, we submit, should be a way of empowering consumers. It should not become one more way in which producers can get away with inferior goods by preying on our limited ability to process perception information. But more often than not, research flows where the money is, and if the money comes from producers and not from consumers, then consumers have to work doubly hard to reach their own conclusions from the evidence presented. They need to use these sorts of findings—and we hope our distillation of those is helpful in precisely this way—to be empowered in how to avoid the pitfalls.

Knowing more about the reliability of judges allows us to discount appropriately ratings that are bandied about like talismans. Knowing about what can influence a wine purchase decision may by itself offset at the margin whatever unrestrained influence is lurking. Being aware that there is a correlation between the country of origin of music played in a store and wine purchases from that country, you may be more sensitive to what's in the background the next time you pick out that Grüner Veltliner you hadn't planned on buying. This is not a joke, by the way. It's a 1999 study from the *Journal of Applied Psychology*.[58]

We are given a unique chance to become invested and informed consumers, to help shape the wine we wish to enjoy. Let's hold on for dear life and not let this progress be hijacked for the purposes of empty marketing.

# Chapter 9 Drinking games for adults

To try your hand at blind tasting, you don't need to be as obsessive-compulsive as we were when putting together this book. At home, or even at a BYO restaurant, it's fairly easy to blind taste a few wines at a time.

You don't need much to start. Tasting forms for everyday wine drinkers can be downloaded from thewinetrials.com. Brown lunch bags from the supermarket work well to conceal wines, and packing tape does a decent job of sealing them in. Champagne buckets, beach pails, large plastic tumblers, or cocktail shakers will all work as spit buckets; even if you don't plan to spit, you'll need buckets for dumping out remaining wine between tastes.

Beyond that, the key ingredients are wine, lots of paper, pens, patient friends, and matching glasses. (Differently shaped glasses can have different effects on the wine, although this effect has been grossly exaggerated by glassware companies.)

However many wines you want to taste, split your wines into flights to two to six bottles each. Palate fatigue can set in when you hit the seventh or eighth wine, and it's also difficult to rank wines against each other when more than six are involved.

If you're using standard wine glasses, then be sure, at a minimum, that your glasses curve inward at the top and aren't merely cylindrical. But the ideal glasses for blind tasting are 155 mm

ISO tasting glasses, designed by scientists in France to concentrate the aromas at exactly the point where your nose sticks into the glass. They're small enough to fit many on a table, and their tapered shape is also designed to allow for vigorous swirling without spillage. These are the glasses used in many wine industry conventions and fairs, and they are what we used in our blind tastings. You can order ISO-certified tasting glasses at thewinetrials.com.

If you're doing an informal tasting at a party, there are really only four important rules to keep in mind: first, remove the entire foil top on the wine, not just the top of it, as you might normally. Foil can be a dead giveaway. Second, the person who bagged and sealed the wines (with the packing tape around the neck) shouldn't be the same person who numbers the bottles (a Sharpie works best). Third, once the tasting begins, tasters shouldn't be allowed to discuss wines with each other before assigning their ratings—that will introduce serious bias toward the opinions of the more self-confident people in the group. Finally, tasters shouldn't be allowed to change their ratings after the wines have been exposed. That would defeat the whole purpose of the game. Of course, it goes without saying that tasters shouldn't be told anything about the wine they're tasting beforehand—not even the country of origin or grape, and certainly not the price range.

If you want to do a more formal tasting, there are several other things you should keep in mind. First, you should transfer screwcap wines into empty non-screwcap bottles to avoid bias, because the threads will be visible even after the wine is brown-bagged. Magnums, jug wines, and box wines should also be transferred to normal 750 mL bottles in the same way.

Unless you're tasting older vintages, wines should be left uncorked for a minimum of 45 minutes before serving to let them breathe and minimize oxygen reduction that can taint wine aromas, particularly with screwcap wines. White wines should be tasted at around 55°F to 60°F (13°C to 16°C), somewhat above the temperature at which you would normally drink them; it's easier to tell the difference between wines when they're warmer. In general, taking whites from the refrigerator, opening them, and leaving them to breathe at room temperature for about 30 minutes should do the trick. Red wines should be tasted around 60°F to 65°F (16°C to 18°C).

With respect to pouring wines, there are two methods that work, depending on how many glasses you have. The method that best allows for wine-against-wine comparison is to distribute one glass for each wine to each taster, and to pour all the wines at once. So if you had four tasters and six wines, you'd need 24 glasses. (If you don't have a dishwasher, you'll hate this method.)

The second method, which is more suitable for large numbers of people, is to give the tasters one glass each and let them pour wines themselves as they go. In that case, after tasting each wine, tasters should rinse their glasses with the next wine to be tasted before pouring the actual tasting portion. When rinsing, tasters should make an effort to coat the whole inside surface of the glass with the new wine while holding the glass upside down over the spit bucket and slowly pouring it out. Once the glass is coated, tasters can then pour a full tasting portion of the next wine.

When the wines are served, every taster should be given a rating form and a pen. Serve plain water crackers (Carr's plain flavor is reliably neutral) at the table to cleanse the palate between wines. Some people like to drink water between wines as well, although it's not as good a palate cleanser as crackers.

Encourage tasters to pour two-ounce tasting portions, to take at most one swallow of each wine, and to spit on repeated tastes. (Very few people will get wasted on six swallows of wine, and some people—I'm on the fence—feel that something is lost on the finish if you don't swallow at least once.) If tasters are tempted to drink more than that, remind them that once the tasting is finished and the bottles are exposed, they can drink as much as they want.

Encourage your tasters to taste the wines in random order. It's well established that tasters have a positive bias towards the first item tasted or rated in a series, and in our tastings we took steps to ensure that tasters did not all taste in the same order.

Tasters should both rate and rank the wines. Ranking is a more accurate way of scoring wines against each other, because it forces tasters to make tough decisions, but rating is the best way to compare wines from one flight or tasting to wines from another. Our rating scale is intentionally simple, and we have four rating check boxes—as opposed to five—so that tasters are forced to make the tough decision between the second and third, rather than falling back on an indecisive middle choice. Accordingly, you should not allow tasters to check between boxes.

When all the tasters are done rating, make it clear that people are no longer allowed to make changes to their forms, and then, with great fanfare and drama, expose the wines. Don't forget to immediately record which wine corresponds to which bag number. The simplest way of scoring the wines is called a "rank sum": you add up all the tasters' rankings, and the lowest score wins. To calculate a total rating, count one point for every bad vote, two for okay, three for good, four for great, and the highest score wins.

And remember, above all else, that even a taster under the influence of alcohol is better than a taster under the influence of others—or of the label.

# **Notes** on Part I

1. Winning wines from the previous edition of *The Wine Trials* were grandfathered into the tastings, allowing them to bypass the nomination process and defend their titles regardless of this year's case production numbers or whether they were re-nominated by industry professionals. Once entered into the blind tastings, though, these previous winners received no special consideration.

2. Economists often use logarithmic price scales to analyze wine pricing, as we did; this helps to test the hypothesis that a wine's price might increase exponentially as its quality increases linearly.

3. Some people in the wine industry dispute the validity of tasting cheap wines against expensive wines, objecting that the former are generally easier to enjoy on their own, while the latter need to be served with food and/or need to age for several years. See Chapter 7 for a discussion on the question of reviewing wine paired with food. However, controlled wine tastings have long been the accepted industry standard for the evaluation of wines at any price range. As for the question of age, older vintages of expensive wines are rarely available at most wine stores or restaurants, so they would not properly represent the wines people are actually

buying and drinking. Tasting older wines would also increase the likelihood of many other confounding factors, including improper storage, oxidation, and cork taint.

4. For a thought-provoking argument against the use of statistical significance and p-value thresholds to show the validity (or lack thereof) of an experimental result, see Deirdre McCloskey's *The Cult of Statistical Significance: How the Standard Error Costs Us Jobs, Justice, and Lives* (University of Michigan Press, 2006).

5. Robin Goldstein, Johan Almenberg, Anna Dreber, Alexis Herschkowitsch, and Jacob Katz, "Do More Expensive Wines Taste Better? Evidence from a Large Sample of US Blind Tastings," *Journal of Wine Economics,* Vol. 3, No. 1 (Spring 2008).

6. Jancis Robinson, *Confessions of a Wine Lover* (Penguin Books, 1997).

7. Maynard Amerine and Edward Roessler, *Wines: Their Sensory Evaluation* (W.H. Freeman and Company, 1976).

8. Sébastien Lecocq and Michael Visser, "What Determines Wine Prices: Objective vs. Sensory Characteristics," *Journal of Wine Economics*, Vol. 1, No. 1 (Spring 2006).

9. When I refer to "Champagne," I mean only wines that come from the French Champagne appellation, which are rarely available for less than $25 and are often far more expensive than that.

10. Frédéric Brochet, "Chemical Object Representation in the Field of Consciousness" (application presented for the Grand Prix of the Académie Amorim following work carried out towards a doctorate from the Faculty of Oenology of Bordeaux, General Oenology Laboratory), 2001.

11. Ralph Allison and Kenneth Uhl, "Influence of Beer Brand Identification on Taste Perception," *Journal of Marketing Research,* Vol. 1, No. 3 (August 1964).

12. Robin Goldstein, Seamus Campbell, Johan Almenberg, and Anna Dreber, "Can people distinguish between different brands of

European pale lager beer?" In prep, presented at the annual meeting of the American Association of Wine Economists, Davis, CA, June 2010.

13. Leonard Lee, Shane Frederick, and Dan Ariely, "Try It, You'll Like It: The Influence of Expectation, Consumption, and Revelation on Preferences for Beer," *Psychological Science*, Vol. 17, No. 12 (December 2006).

14. Hilke Plassmann, John O'Doherty, Baba Shiv, and Antonio Rangel, "Marketing Actions Can Modulate Neural Representations of Experienced Pleasantness," *Proceedings of the National Academy of Sciences* (January 14, 2008), http://www.pnas.org/cgi/content/abstract/0706929105v1.

15. Statistics were taken from custom searches for wines $10 and under from the 2000 to 2007 vintages performed on both www.winespectator.com (subscribers only) and www.wineenthusiast.com (open to the public). 1,953 wines returned by the *Wine Enthusiast* search with prices listed as $0 were ignored.

16. Roman Weil, "Analysis of Reserve and Regular Bottlings: Why Pay for a Difference Only the Critics Claim to Notice?" *Chance*, Vol. 18, No. 3 (Summer 2005).

17. Tyler Colman, Dr. Vino blog, "Changes at the *Wine Advocate*? Correspondence with Parker and Miller," http://www.drvino.com/2009/04/16/changes-at-the-wine-advocate-correspondence-with-parker-and-miller (April 16, 2009).

18. Robin Goldstein, Blind Taste blog, "What Does It Take To Get a Wine Spectator Award of Excellence?", http://blindtaste.com/2008/08/15/what-does-it-take-to-get-a-wine-spectator-award-of-excellence (August 15, 2008).

19. James Laube, Laube Unfined Blog, "When Tasting, Blind Offers Vision," www.winespectator.com/Wine/Blogs/Blog_Detail/0,4211,1426,00.html (October 4, 2007).

20. The website is not clear on how specific the regions or appellations with which *Wine Spectator* critics are provided prior to tasting, so I don't know if they're told the wine is from its specific appellation, "Hermitage," or the more general region "Northern Rhône." However, Hermitage is listed on Spectator's wine review search page as one of the "Wine Regions," so it seems reasonable to assume that it fits into their definition of "region."

21. See, for instance K.A. Lattey, B.R. Bramley, and I.L. Francis "Consumer acceptability, sensory properties and expert quality judgments of Australian Cabernet Sauvignon and Shiraz wines," *Australian Journal of Grape and Wine Research*, Vol. 16, No. 189 (2010).

22. S. Mueller, P. Osidacz, L. Francis, L. Lockshin, "The relative importance of extrinsic and intrinsic wine attributes: Combining discrete choice and informed sensory consumer testing," Refereed paper, 5th International Conference of the Academy of Wine Business Research, February 2001, Auckland, New Zealand.

23. Gérard Liger-Belair, Clara Cilindre, Régis D. Gougeon, Marianna Lucio, Istvan Gebefügi, Philippe Jeandet, and Philippe Schmitt-Kopplin, "Unraveling different chemical fingerprints between a champagne wine and its aerosols," Proceedings of the National Academy of Sciences.

24. LVMH 2007 Annual Report, available online at http://www.lvmh.com/comfi/pdf_gbr/LVMH2007AnnualReport.pdf.

25. Constellation 2007 Annual Report, available online at http://library.corporate-ir.net/library/85/851/85116/items/252600/STZ_2007AR.pdf.

26. Business Wire. "Excellent First Half of the Year for LVMH," July 27, 2010. www.forbes.com/feeds/businesswire/2010/07/27/businesswire143007424.html

27. Justin Weinberg, "Taste How Expensive This Is," in *Wine & Philosophy: A Symposium on Thinking and Drinking*, ed. Fritz Allhoff (Blackwell Publishing, 2008).

28. Hilke Plassmann, John O'Doherty, Baba Shiv, and Antonio Rangel, "Marketing Actions Can Modulate Neural Representations of Experienced Pleasantness," *Proceedings of the National Academy of Sciences* (January 14, 2008), http://www.pnas.org/cgi/content/abstract/0706929105v1.

29. Miles Thomas, "On Vines and Minds," The Psychologist (British Psychological Society magazine), Vol. 21, No. 5 (May 2008).

30. "Hitting the spot," *The Economist*, January 17, 2008.

31. Annick Vignes and Olivier Gergaud, "Twilight of the Idols in the Market for Champagne: Dissonance or Consonance in Consumer Preferences?" *Journal of Wine Research*, Vol. 13, No. 3 (2007).

32. Eric Asimov, The Pour, "If I Only Knew When I Tasted It…" http://thepour.blogs.nytimes.com/2007/09/13/if-i-only-knew-when-i-tasted-it/ (September 13, 2007).

33. Eric Asimov, The Pour, "Judging the Judging," http://thepour.blogs.nytimes.com/2007/09/17/judging-the-judging/ (September 17, 2007).

34. Eric Asimov, The Pour, "A Closer Look at 'The Wine Trials,'" http://http://thepour.blogs.nytimes.com/2008/04/22/a-closer-look-at-the-wine-trials/ (April 22, 2008).

35. Eric Asimov, "Wine's Pleasures: Are They All In Your Head?" *New York Times*, May 7, 2008.

36. Héla Hadj Ali, Sébastien Lecocq, and Michael Visser, "The Impact of Gurus: Parker Grades and *En Primeur* Wine Prices," *The Economic Journal*, Vol. 118, No. 529 (2008).

37. The "New World" designation also traditionally includes wines from Chile, Argentina, New Zealand, and South Africa, and the "Old World" designation generally includes all of Europe.

38. K.A. Lattey, B.R. Bramley, and I.L. Francis "Consumer acceptability, sensory properties and expert quality judgments of Australian Cabernet Sauvignon and Shiraz wines," *Australian Journal of Grape and Wine Research*, Vol. 16, No. 189 (2010).

39. Robin Goldstein, book review of *Parker's Wine Bargains: The World's Greatest Wine Values Under $25* by Robert M. Parker, *Journal of Wine Economics*, Vol. 5, No. 1, pages 22-29 (2010).

40. Domenic V. Cicchetti and Arnold F. Cicchetti, "Wine rating scales: Assessing their utility for producers, consumers, and oenologic researchers," International Journal of Wine Research, Vol. 1, pages 73-83 (2009).

41. Frank J. Prial, "The Wallaby That Roared Across the Wine Industry," *New York Times* (April 23, 2006).

42. Elin McCoy, *The Emperor of Wine: The Rise of Robert M. Parker, Jr., and the Reign of American Taste* (Ecco, 2005).

43. Diego Begalli, Lara Agnoli, and Stefano Codurri "Preferenze dei consumatori per i vini a denominazione di origine: un'analisi qualitativa nella realtà del Veneto," *Economia e Diritto Agroalimentare*, Vol. XIV, No. 2 (2009).

44. Posted by Karl Storchmann, "Biased Wine Reviews? A Response from *Wine Spectator*" December 11, 2009.

45. Jonathan Reuter, "Does Advertising Bias Product Reviews? An Analysis of Wine Ratings," *Journal of Wine Economics*, Vol. 4, No. 2 (Winter 2009).

46. Robin Goldstein, Blind Taste, "New study suggests that Wine Spectator advertisers get higher ratings," http://blindtaste.com/2009/12/10/new-study-suggests-that-wine-spectator-advertisers-get-higher-ratings (10 December 2009).

47. Robin Goldstein, Johan Almenberg, Anna Dreber, Alexis Herschkowitsch, and Jacob Katz, "Do More Expensive Wines Taste Better? Evidence from a Large Sample of US Blind Tastings," *Journal of Wine Economics*, Vol. 3, No. 1 (Spring 2008).

48. Robert T. Hodgson, "An Analysis of the Concordance Among 13 U.S. Wine Competitions," *Journal of Wine Economics*, Vol. 4, No. 1 (Spring 2009).

49. Richard Gawel and Peter W. Godden, "Evaluation of the consistency of wine quality assessments from expert wine tasters," *Journal of Grape and Wine Research,* Volume 14, No. 1 (2008).

50. Robert T. Hodgson, "An Examination of Judge Reliability at a major U.S. Wine Competition," *Journal of Wine Economics*, Vol. 3, No. 2 (Fall 2008).

52. Robert T. Hodgson, "How Expert are 'Expert' Wine Judges?," *Journal of Wine Economics*, Vol. 4, No. 2 (abstract) (Winter 2009).

53. Diego Begalli, Lara Agnoli, and Stefano Codurri "Preferenze dei consumatori per i vini a denominazione di origine: un'analisi qualitativa nella realtà del Veneto," *Economia e Diritto Agroalimentare*, Vol. XIV, No. 2 (2009).

53. Annick Vignes and Olivier Gergaud, "Twilight of the Idols in the Market for Champagne: Dissonance or Consonance in Consumer Preferences?," *Journal of Wine Research*, Vol. 18, No. 3 (2007).

54. Luiz de Mello and Ricardo Pires, "Message on the Bottle: Colours and Shapes of Wine Labels," American Association of Wine Economists Working Paper No. 42 (September 2009).

55. K.A. Lattey, B.R. Bramley, and I.L. Francis, "Consumer acceptability, sensory properties and expert quality judgements of Australian Cabernet Sauvignon and Shiraz wines," *Australian Journal of Grape and Wine Research*, Vol. 16, No. 1 (2010).

56. Ramo Barrena and Mercedes Sanchez, "Connecting product attributes with emotional benefits: Analysis of a Mediterranean product across consumer age segments," *British Food Journal*, Vol. 111, No. 2 (2009).

57. S. Mueller, P. Osidacz, L. Francis, and L. Lockshin, "The relative importance of extrinsic and intrinsic wine attributes: Combining discrete choice and informed sensory consumer testing," Refereed paper, 5th International Conference of the Academy of Wine Business Research, February 2001, Auckland, New Zealand.

58. North, A.C., Hargreaves, D.J. & McKendrick, J., "The influence of in-store music on wine selections," *Journal of Applied Psychology*, 84, 271–276 (1999).

**Part II** The 2011 Wine Trials
*by Alexis Herschkowitsch
with Tyce Walters*

# Chapter 10 About the 2011 trials

In the pages that follow, the *Wine Trials* editors review the 175 winners of this year's trials—the top-scoring wines under $15 from our brown-bag blind tastings of the new releases for 2011. (For more on our selection process, please see the preface.)

The United States is the most-represented region in the book, with 49 of the 175 winners, of which 34 are from California and 15 are from Washington State. We're huge fans of Oregon wines, but Willamette Valley Pinot Noir, one of America's most reliable appellations, rarely dips below $15.

Last year we were delighted by the changing style of California Chardonnays, and their move away from the oak-bomb style and toward better balance and bright acidity. That trend has held, and we'd like to think it's spreading: this year's winner in the Heavy White category was Australia's Yalumba Unwooded Chard, which our blind tasters loved for its bright citrus and apple flavors. See, great things can be done without oak chips!

Still, for all the fanfare about Australia, its wines only comprise 7 of our 175 recommendations this year. As a whole, the wines still tend to be too alcoholic, over-extracted, and in a few cases our blind tasters were turned off by strong sulfur aromas.

We were pleasantly surprised by the strong showing from some more obscure regions this year. Bulgaria had three wines among our winners, and Turkey had two bottles worth recommending. In both countries the tradition of winemaking is long, but the practice of exporting and marketing to an international audience is not. And it certainly shows—these bottles (especially the Turkish ones) are not designed to catch consumers' eyes. But the contents caught our blind tasters' palates.

There are some impressive sweeter things among this year's selections. Germany's Dr. L Riesling was the winner in the sweet/aromatic category, and it's delightful: mineral, apricot, honey, apple, and all for $12. Bulgaria's Targovishte is another bottle to keep an eye on.

As for the Old World heavyweights, Italy and France came in with 20 and 18 wines, respectively, in the top 175. The weakening euro has been a positive thing for American consumers looking for value from Europe, especially southern Europe, although on the flip side, the economic crisis in Greece and a brewing situation in Italy does not bode well for the commercial prospects of some wine producers. Austria managed to edge in with a couple of Grüner Veltliners, and we'd love to see more, but higher prices and lower production continued to keep many bottles out of this guide's scope.

Spain wowed our blind tasters once again with 23 wines recommended in this year's edition. Cavas were universally loved for their crisp flavors and delicate bubbles. Rioja, as usual, contributed a few winners whose elegance and age betrayed their under-$15 price point. New to the guide this year are some lovely Spanish whites: a sharp Albariño from Rias Baixas and a sleek Verdejo-Viura blend from Rueda. Portugal again got accolades for its sprightly, summery, staggeringly inexpensive Vinhos Verdes.

Down south, Argentina and Chile continue to defend their reputations as good regions for value wines, with 23 wines in total making it into this year's edition. Still, the range of wines coming out of the southern cone is quite large, so this translates to a lower hit rate: the American market has been so flooded with cheap South American wines that an increasing number of problematic wines, especially flawed mass-produced Chilean bottles with burnt rubber characteristics, have worked their way onto the marketplace. Proceed with caution.

And congratulations are in order for South Africa. After not having a single winner last year, the country this year has four wines in our guide. Three are lovely Chenin Blancs, including the silky Backsberg bottling. The token South African red came from Man Vintners, who also contributed a Chenin Blanc.

Of course, if you've taken this book seriously so far, then you'll take our blind tasting results with a grain of salt. To some extent, these choices might reflect the preferences of wine experts more than those of wine novices, as the Wine Trials editors all have plenty of experience with wine. (That said, tasters for the final round, in which the "Best of the Wine Trials" winners were chosen, were a mix of experts and everyday wine drinkers.)

It bears mention that there are many excellent values under $15 from smaller producers that unfortunately did not meet our criteria for widespread availability. That's why it's doubly important to work toward creating your own top 175. In a sophisticated wine store, the best place to start is often with the wines you haven't heard of—not because wines from obscure regions or producers are necessarily better, but because you're not paying a premium for a name-brand region or producer. A good wine store employee can be more helpful than a magazine critic. But nothing can substitute for taking the wine home and blind-tasting it yourself against other wines.

You'll notice that, unlike the rest of the book, the reviews are written in first-person plural ("we"); that's because they represent a joint effort between Robin Goldstein, Alexis Herschkowitsch, Tyce Walters, and the rest of our blind tasting panel. In general, we tried to highlight sensory notes that were shared by multiple blind tasters, not just one taster's flight of fancy, although the latter was sometimes so amusing that we couldn't help ourselves. (Some good comments didn't make it in the book because the wine didn't qualify, like one taster's succinct description of Sutter Home White Zinfandel: "If Jesus tasted this wine, he'd turn it back to water.")

After the wines were revealed, we also added non-blind portions of review text discussing the producer, grapes, bottle design, and so on; but we did not change any tasting notes or descriptions, nor did we change any decisions about which wines would be included.

"Heavy" vs. "light" is a subjective distinction, to be sure, but one we hope you'll get used to; roughly speaking, it corresponds with alcohol content, thickness of texture, intensity of flavor, and what wine people call "body," but that doesn't fully capture the distinction. There are also special categories for rosé, sparkling wines, and sweet or aromatic wines.

In our reviews, we've tried to use everyday language to describe the wines—adjectives that will make sense to everyday wine drinkers. We do use fruit flavors, of course; the English language doesn't really have any way of describing taste sensations without making reference to other taste sensations, the way it does for colors. But we've done our best to stick to familiar flavors. We'll talk about orange or grapefruit, not boxwood bud or pencil lead.

The only two wine buzzwords that we use consistently are "tannins" and "acidity." Tannins are the quality (found almost exclusively in red wines) that dry out the mouth; acidity is the opposite, the quality that makes your mouth water. We also review the design of each bottle, a practice that has invited criticism from some, accolades from others; while we always invite feedback, positive or negative, we are baffled by the response from some people that a wine's bottle design is not worthy of critique. First of all, the scientific evidence in the first part of this book has shown that we all respond strongly to what a bottle looks like—so strongly, in fact, that it can even affect the taste of the wine on a basic level. This makes bottle design start to look more like an intrinsic characteristic of wine as a consumer product, and less like an extrinsic one. Whether you're bringing a bottle to a party or staring at it over dinner, the bottle and label are part of what you're buying, experiencing, enjoying or hating—why not evaluate them as such?

The average retail price in the book is found in a circle in the upper right-hand corner of the page. A white circle means a white wine, a red circle means a red wine, and a gray circle means a rosé. Sparkling wines have bubbles coming out of a white circle. Each review page also specifies the wine's region, vintage tasted, suggested food pairings (which are utterly subjective, of course), and grape varieties. Websites are listed, too.

Speaking of grape varieties, you might be wondering why we don't categorize wines on that axis, as many wine guides do. There's a reason for this: our view is that, especially for inexpensive wines, categorization by grape variety can often be misleading and unhelpful. Certainly, in some cases, varieties do influence the taste of the wine—especially extremely acidic grapes like Sauvignon Blanc, or sweet or aromatic grapes like Muscat or Gewürztraminer—but in inexpensive wines, this effect is often minimal compared with the Old World-New World divide or the light-heavy style difference. For example, a Merlot from Bordeaux would probably tend to taste more like a Cabernet Sauvignon from Bordeaux than like a Merlot from the United States. (If you're unconvinced by this argument, you can look wines up by grape variety in the index beginning on page 220.)

Even if you do not agree with all of our selections, we hope that our results will serve, at least, as a useful starting point for your own blind tasting journey. We also hope you'll question your assumptions about wine pricing, hold blind-tasting parties with your friends, and ultimately, join us in helping to restore the kind of order to the market that might only come from a grassroots movement of consumers that make a conscious decision to trust their own palates more than price tags.

# **Chapter 11** Winners of the 2011 trials

| **2011 Wine of the Year** | Country | Price |
|---|---|---|
| Dr. L Riesling | Germany | $12 |

| **2011 Winery of the Year** | Country | |
|---|---|---|
| Château Ste. Michelle | USA (WA) | |

| **Best of the Wine Trials winners** | Country | Price |
|---|---|---|
| **Sparkling** J.P. Chenet Blanc de Blancs Brut | France | $12 |
| **Light white** Bogle Sauvignon Blanc | USA (CA) | $9 |
| **Heavy white** Yalumba Unwooded Chard | Australia | $10 |
| **Rosé** Lâl Rosé | Turkey | $10 |
| **Light red** Monte Antico | Italy | $12 |
| **Heavy red** Doña Paula Los Cardos Malbec | Argentina | $12 |
| **Sweet/aromatic** Dr. L Riesling | Germany | $12 |

| **Best of the Wine Trials finalists** | Country | Price |
|---|---|---|
| Alamos Torrontés | Argentina | $13 |
| Campo Viejo Rioja Reserva *light red* | Spain | $11 |
| Cerro Bercial *light red* | Spain | $11 |
| Château Ste. Michelle Sauv. Blanc *light white* | USA (WA) | $10 |
| Château Ste. Michelle Syrah *heavy red* | USA (WA) | $13 |
| Columbia Crest Two Vines Riesling *aromatic* | USA (WA) | $8 |
| Concannon Petite Sirah *heavy red* | USA (CA) | $15 |

*continues on next page*

**Best of the Wine Trials finalists** *continued*

| | Country | Price |
|---|---|---|
| Domaine Ste. Michelle Brut *sparkling* | USA (WA) | $12 |
| El Coto de Rioja Crianza *light red* | Spain | $12 |
| Freixenet Carta Nevada Brut *sparkling* | Spain | $9 |
| Gabbiano Chianti Classico *light red* | Italy | $12 |
| Kourtaki Mavrodaphne of Patras *sweet* | Greece | $10 |
| Opala Vinho Verde *light white* | Portugal | $9 |
| René Barbier Mediterranean Red *light red* | Spain | $6 |
| Ruffino Chianti DOCG *light red* | Italy | $12 |
| 35° South Sauvignon Blanc *light white* | Chile | $9 |
| Trivento Reserve Torrontés *aromatic* | Argentina | $12 |
| Vieux Papes Rouge *light red* | France | $6 |

**Best bargains**

| | Country | Price |
|---|---|---|
| Alice White Chardonnay *heavy white* | Australia | $7 |
| Aveleda Fonte Vinho Verde *light white* | Portugal | $7 |
| Barefoot Sauvignon Blanc *light white* | USA (CA) | $7 |
| Black Box Cabernet Sauvignon *heavy red* | USA (CA) | $5 |
| Diflora Chianti 365 *light red* | Italy | $7 |
| Fonseca Twin Vines Vinho Verde *light white* | Portugal | $7 |
| Foxhorn Chardonnay *heavy white* | USA (CA) | $6 |
| Fuzelo Vinho Verde *light white* | Portugal | $7 |
| Gato Negro Malbec *heavy red* | Chile | $6 |
| Monthaven Merlot *light red* | USA (CA) | $6 |
| René Barbier Mediterranean Red *light red* | Spain | $6 |
| René Barbier Mediterranean White *light white* | Spain | $6 |
| Vieux Papes Blanc de Blancs *light white* | France | $6 |
| Vieux Papes Rouge *light red* | France | $6 |

## All *Wine Trials 2011* winners

**Sparkling**

| | Country | Price |
|---|---|---|
| Aria Estate Brut | Spain | $12 |
| Barefoot Bubbly Brut Cuvée | USA (CA) | $10 |
| Barefoot Bubbly Extra Dry | USA (CA) | $10 |
| Borgo Magredo Extra Dry Prosecco | Italy | $15 |
| Casteller Cava | Spain | $13 |
| Casteller Cava Rosé | Spain | $10 |
| Domaine Ste. Michelle Blanc de Noirs | USA (WA) | $12 |
| Domaine Ste. Michelle Brut | USA (WA) | $12 |
| Freixenet Carta Nevada Brut | Spain | $9 |
| Freixenet Cordon Negro Brut | Spain | $12 |

| **Sparkling** *continued* | *Country* | *Price* |
|---|---|---|
| Freixenet Cordon Negro Extra Dry | Spain | $9 |
| J.P. Chenet Blanc de Blancs Brut | France | $12 |
| Mionetto Il Prosecco | Italy | $10 |
| Zardetto Prosecco | Italy | $14 |

| **Light Old World white** | *Country* | *Price* |
|---|---|---|
| Aveleda Fonte Vinho Verde | Portugal | $7 |
| Belleruche Côtes-du-Rhône Blanc | France | $13 |
| Çankaya | Turkey | $11 |
| Casal Garcia Vinho Verde | Portugal | $9 |
| Château La Gravière Blanc | France | $8 |
| Condes de Albarei Albariño | Spain | $12 |
| Domäne Wachau Grüner Veltliner | Austria | $15 |
| Fonseca Twin Vines Vinho Verde | Portugal | $7 |
| Fumées Blanches | France | $11 |
| Fuzelo Vinho Verde | Portugal | $7 |
| Gobelsburger Grüner Veltliner | Austria | $13 |
| Mania Rueda | Spain | $14 |
| Opala Vinho Verde | Portugal | $9 |
| Oro de Castilla | Spain | $14 |
| Principessa Gavia | Italy | $14 |
| Quinta da Aveleda Vinho Verde | Portugal | $9 |
| Quinta da Romeira | Portugal | $11 |
| René Barbier Mediterranean White | Spain | $6 |
| Ruffino Lumina | Italy | $13 |
| Targovishte Sauvignon Blanc | Bulgaria | $9 |
| Vieux Papes Blanc de Blancs | France | $6 |
| Villa Wolf Pinot Gris | Germany | $12 |
| Vinha da Defesa | Portugal | $13 |

| **Heavy Old World white** | *Country* | *Price* |
|---|---|---|
| Cave de Lugny Mâcon-Villages | France | $11 |
| Guigal Côtes du Rhône | France | $13 |
| La Vieille Ferme Blanc | France | $8 |

| **Light New World white** | *Country* | *Price* |
|---|---|---|
| Araucano Sauvignon Blanc | Chile | $13 |
| Barefoot Sauvignon Blanc | USA (CA) | $7 |
| Bogle Sauvignon Blanc | USA (CA) | $9 |
| Brancott Sauvignon Blanc | New Zealand | $13 |
| Château Ste. Michelle Horse Heaven SB | USA (WA) | $15 |
| Château Ste. Michelle Sauvignon Blanc | USA (WA) | $10 |

## Light New World white *continued*

| | Country | Price |
|---|---|---|
| Cycles Gladiator Pinot Grigio | USA (CA) | $10 |
| Geyser Peak Sauvignon Blanc | USA (CA) | $14 |
| Hogue Cellars Pinot Grigio | USA (WA) | $10 |
| Lurton Pinot Gris | Argentina | $10 |
| Mohua Sauvignon Blanc | New Zealand | $13 |
| Nobilo Sauvignon Blanc | New Zealand | $14 |
| Oyster Bay Sauvignon Blanc | New Zealand | $13 |
| Root: 1 Sauvignon Blanc | Chile | $13 |
| Santa Ema Sauvignon Blanc | Chile | $10 |
| Starborough Sauvignon Blanc | New Zealand | $13 |
| 35° South Sauvignon Blanc | Chile | $9 |
| Villa Maria Sauvignon Blanc | New Zealand | $15 |
| Viña Los Vascos Sauvignon Blanc | Chile | $11 |
| Yalumba Unwooded Chardonnay | Australia | $10 |

## Heavy New World white

| | Country | Price |
|---|---|---|
| Alice White Chardonnay | Australia | $7 |
| Foxhorn Chardonnay | USA (CA) | $6 |
| Santa Ema Chardonnay | Chile | $10 |
| Woodbridge Chardonnay | USA (CA) | $8 |

## Rosé

| | Country | Price |
|---|---|---|
| Aimé Roquesante Rosé | France | $13 |
| Banfi Centine Rosé | Italy | $13 |
| Belleruche Côtes-du-Rhône Rosé | France | $13 |
| Casal Garcia Vinho Verde Rosé | Portugal | $8 |
| Lâl Rosé | Turkey | $10 |
| Madame Fleur Rosé | France | $8 |
| Valleclaro Rosado | Spain | $13 |

## Light Old World red

| | Country | Price |
|---|---|---|
| Bohigas Crianza | Spain | $15 |
| Campo Viejo Rioja Reserva | Spain | $11 |
| Cerro Bercial | Spain | $11 |
| Charamba Douro | Portugal | $8 |
| Cortijo Rioja | Spain | $10 |
| Diflora Chianti 365 | Italy | $7 |
| Eder Joven | Spain | $13 |
| El Albar Barricas | Spain | $13 |
| El Coto de Rioja Crianza | Spain | $12 |
| Gabbiano Chianti Classico | Italy | $12 |
| Lan Rioja Crianza | Spain | $12 |

## Light Old World red *continued*

| | Country | Price |
|---|---|---|
| Louis Latour Le Pinot Noir | France | $15 |
| Lungarotti Fiamme | Italy | $14 |
| Malenchini Chianti | Italy | $11 |
| Marqués de Cáceres Rioja | Spain | $15 |
| MontAsolo Merlot | Italy | $8 |
| Monte Antico | Italy | $12 |
| Montecillo Rioja Crianza | Spain | $12 |
| René Barbier Mediterranean Red | Spain | $6 |
| Ruffino Chianti | Italy | $12 |
| Ruffino Chianti Superiore | Italy | $13 |
| San Lorenzo Chianti | Italy | $12 |
| Turning Leaf Pinot Noir | Italy | $8 |
| Vieux Papes Rouge | France | $6 |

## Heavy Old World red

| | Country | Price |
|---|---|---|
| Almira Los Dos | Spain | $8 |
| Belleruche Côtes-du-Rhône Rouge | France | $13 |
| Château Damase | France | $12 |
| Il Rosso di Enzo | Italy | $10 |
| Lagaria Merlot | Italy | $10 |
| Les Hauts de Janeil Syrah Grenache | France | $13 |
| Quinta da Cabriz | Portugal | $11 |
| Umani Ronchi Sangiovese | Italy | $10 |
| VINI Cabernet Sauvignon | Bulgaria | $8 |

## Light New World red

| | Country | Price |
|---|---|---|
| Bogle Pinot Noir | USA (CA) | $13 |
| Cycles Gladiator Pinot Noir | USA (CA) | $14 |
| Jacob's Creek Reserve Pinot Noir | Australia | $14 |
| Man Vintners Cabernet Sauvignon | South Africa | $11 |
| Mark West Pinot Noir | USA (CA) | $11 |
| Matua Pinot Noir | New Zealand | $14 |
| Monthaven Merlot | USA (CA) | $6 |
| Robert Mondavi Pinot Noir | USA (CA) | $11 |
| Washington Hills Merlot | USA (WA) | $10 |

## Heavy New World red

| | Country | Price |
|---|---|---|
| Adobe Red | USA (CA) | $14 |
| Alamos Malbec | Argentina | $10 |
| Aquinas Cabernet Sauvignon | USA (CA) | $15 |
| Argento Bonarda | Argentina | $13 |
| Beringer Cabernet Sauvignon | USA (CA) | $11 |

| Heavy New World red *continued* | Country | Price |
|---|---|---|
| Big House Red | USA (CA) | $8 |
| Black Box Cabernet Sauvignon | USA (CA) | $5 |
| Black Swan Shiraz | Australia | $8 |
| Bogle Cabernet Sauvignon | USA (CA) | $11 |
| Bogle Old Vine Zin | USA (CA) | $11 |
| Bogle Petite Sirah | USA (CA) | $11 |
| Bonterra Cabernet Sauvignon | USA (CA) | $15 |
| Casillero del Diablo Cabernet Sauvignon | Chile | $12 |
| Château Ste. Michelle Syrah | USA (WA) | $13 |
| Columbia Crest Grand Estates Cab | USA (WA) | $11 |
| Concannon Petite Sirah | USA (CA) | $15 |
| Cono Sur Bicycle Cabernet Sauvignon | Chile | $10 |
| Dancing Bull Cabernet Sauvignon | USA (CA) | $12 |
| Doña Paula Los Cardos Malbec | Argentina | $12 |
| Gato Negro Malbec | Chile | $6 |
| Graffigna Centenario Malbec | Argentina | $13 |
| Green Bridge Zinfandel | USA (CA) | $9 |
| Greg Norman Cabernet Merlot | Australia | $15 |
| Happy Camper Cabernet Sauvignon | USA (CA) | $9 |
| Hayman and Hill Cabernet Sauvignon | USA (CA) | $15 |
| House Wine Red | USA (WA) | $12 |
| J. Lohr Estates Los Osos Merlot | USA (CA) | $15 |
| J. Lohr Estates South Ridge Syrah | USA (CA) | $15 |
| Kaiken Reserve Malbec | Argentina | $14 |
| Norton Cabernet Sauvignon | Argentina | $11 |
| Norton Malbec | Argentina | $11 |
| Parducci Sustainable Red | USA (CA) | $10 |
| Pascual Toso Malbec | Argentina | $13 |
| Rosemount Shiraz | Australia | $10 |
| Santa Julia Cabernet Sauvignon | Argentina | $11 |
| Santa Julia Malbec | Argentina | $10 |
| Seven Daughters Winemakers Blend | USA (CA) | $15 |
| Snoqualmie Whistle Stop Red | USA (WA) | $10 |
| Steakhouse Red | USA (WA) | $13 |
| Toasted Head Cabernet Sauvignon | USA (CA) | $14 |
| Trivento Reserve Malbec | Argentina | $12 |
| Waterbrook Mélange Noir | USA (WA) | $15 |
| Yalumba Shiraz Viognier | Australia | $10 |

## Sweet or aromatic

| | Country | Price |
|---|---|---|
| Alamos Torrontés | Argentina | $13 |
| Backsberg Chenin Blanc | South Africa | $12 |
| Big House White | USA (CA) | $8 |
| Columbia Crest Two Vines Riesling | USA (WA) | $8 |
| Columbia Crest Two Vines Vineyard 10 | USA (WA) | $8 |
| Domaine des Salices Viognier | France | $12 |
| Dr. L Riesling | Germany | $12 |
| Estancia Riesling | USA (CA) | $12 |
| Gentil Hugel | France | $15 |
| Kourtaki Mavrodaphne of Patras | Greece | $10 |
| Man VIntners Chenin Blanc | South Africa | $11 |
| Oggi Pinot Grigio | Italy | $9 |
| Pölka Dot Riesling | Germany | $12 |
| Samos Muscat | Greece | $12 |
| Sebeka Chenin Blanc | South Africa | $8 |
| Targovishte Riesling | Bulgaria | $9 |
| Trivento Reserve Torrontés | Argentina | $12 |
| Villa Wolf Dry Riesling | Germany | $12 |
| Washington Hills Late Harvest Riesling | USA (WA) | $10 |

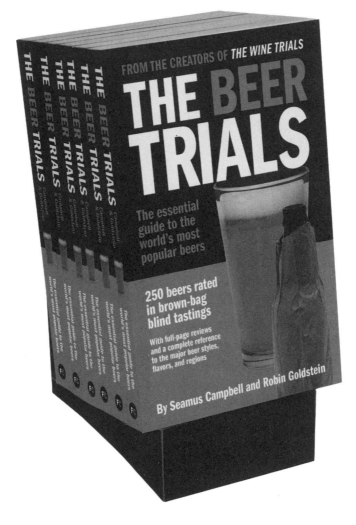

# 2011 wine reviews

# Adobe Red

Clayhouse Wines

**$10**

**Style** Heavy New World red  **Country** USA (CA)
**Vintage tasted** 2008  **Grapes** Zinfandel, Syrah, Petite Sirah,
Malbec, Cabernet Sauvignon, Petit Verdot, Tempranillo, Merlot
**Drink with** hearty beef stews, grilled mushrooms
**Website** www.clayhousewines.com

The grapes in this hearty wine read like a laundry list of the great New World red varietals. Zinfandel, Petite Sirah, and Syrah (under its Aussie name of Shiraz) all reached their apogee—or at least intense notoriety—far from Europe. So it's hardly surprising that this blend should be big, juicy, full of oak, and stereotypically New World in style. We have to admit, it's a blast to see how well these New World titans can play together.

**Nose** It's huge and aggressive, with ripe berries, dark chocolate, cola, and even some floral and herbal aromas. Definitely New World.

**Mouth** More red fruit and oak here, along with caramel and toffee. The tannins are quite elegant for a wine this size.

**Design** The text-only label manages to seem extremely cool. Maybe it has something to do with the carefree flow of the faux handwriting.

# Aimé Roquesante Rosé

Côtes de Provence

**Style** Rosé
**Country** France  **Vintage tasted** 2008
**Grapes** Syrah, Grenache, Mourvèdre
**Drink with** fresh shellfish, whole roast branzino
**Website** www.aime-roquesante.com

We always take it as a good sign when a French wine producer's website is only in French; it suggests that concern for marketing (at least across the Atlantic) isn't trumping winemaking. That focus shows: for one thing, this wine is the pale salmon color we like in a rosé, rather than the terrifying neon pink of some wines we tasted. More importantly, the Roquesante manages to balance delicious fruit with refreshing acidity like only a Provençal rosé can. Just try to drink it without imagining Mediterranean beaches. We dare you.

**Nose** It's a light, fresh strawberry—in marked contrast to the synthetic strawberry quality many lesser wines exhibit.

**Mouth** It's full in the mouth, but the sharp acidity makes it feel lean and refreshing.

**Design** The bottle has a beautiful hourglass shape, and you can see the appealing color from a mile away.

# Alamos Malbec

Mendoza • *Three-time Wine Trials selection*

**Style** Heavy New World red
**Country** Argentina  **Vintage tasted** 2009
**Grapes** Malbec
**Drink with** roast beef, roasted eggplant
**Website** www.alamoswines.com

Back for an impressive third time, this crowd-pleasing Argentine Malbec marries rich fruit flavors with dark, earthy notes. The winery states that its team "aims to make wines that are as good as wines twice their price," something at which we think they've succeeded admirably. That might be due in part to their use of a double manual selection process (they go through the grapes twice) to make sure only good ones make it in. That work is time consuming and expensive, but it's definitely reflected in this excellent wine.

**Nose** The rich red fruit, berries, and earthiness are evocative. One taster detected some sulfur, though.

**Mouth** It's silky and elegant, with impressive structure and balance. Our blind tasters were particularly fond of the bold, velvety fruit flavors.

**Design** A dark, heavy, tapered bottle, minimalist writing, and a rugged Andes-scape create a rather imposing look, even if the contents are quite approachable.

# Alamos Torrontés
Cafayate

**Style** Aromatic New World white
**Country** Argentina  **Vintage tasted** 2009
**Grapes** Torrontés
**Drink with** cold shrimp, tuna rolls
**Website** www.alamoswines.com

For the past two years, Alamos' Malbec has been a favorite of our blind tasters; this year it's joined by the floral, fruity Torrontés. So aromatic it could be mistaken for a classy perfume, it should be a hit with anyone looking for that perfect apéritif. It should also be easy to find: it's distributed by the massive E & J Gallo, so there'll always be a bottle handy at a wine store near you.

**Nose** Pear, grapefruit, apricot, and intense floral aromas dominate this impressively aromatic nose.

**Mouth** It's crisp and dry, which contrasts nicely with the floral flavors that persist into the finish.

**Design** The mountain landscape is less effective on this pale bottle than on the Malbec's darker surface. But hey, who doesn't like the Andes?

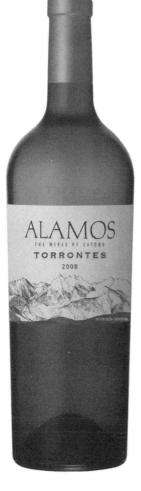

# Alice White Chardonnay

*Three-time Wine Trials selection*

**Style** Heavy New World white
**Country** Australia  **Vintage tasted** 2009
**Grapes** Chardonnay
**Drink with** risotto, fettuccine alfredo
**Website** www.alicewhite.com

We love to hate Australia's irritatingly popular "critter wine" producers, who often seem to spend more time drawing animal cartoons than making decent wine. Alice White's Chardonnay, however, is an exception to the rule—and has been for the last several years. It's big and oaky, unmistakably an Australian Chardonnay, but balanced and quite delicious. Maybe it will make us rethink our stance on kangaroo wines.

**Nose** It's fairly oaky but balanced by some big, lush fruit.

**Mouth** There's still oak, but as one blind taster said, the wine continues to be "nice and tight."

**Design** The marketing team plays off just about every Aussie stereotype, with the kangaroo roasting in the spirally sun. But the pleasantly austere san-serif small-caps font beneath redeems some of the clichés.

# Almira Los Dos

$8

**Style** Heavy Old World red
**Country** Spain  **Vintage tasted** 2008
**Grapes** Garnacha, Syrah
**Drink with** duck breast, pork chops with cranberry sauce

Once again, Spain proves itself as one of the great sources of value wine. This one is made of Garnacha and Syrah—a combination most familiar in the wines of the Rhône. Big, fruity, and spicy, Almira won't win any awards for subtlety, but it's no less delicious for that.

**Nose** Pepper, red fruit, and a slight vegetal quality make up a bold, powerful nose.

**Mouth** It could stand to be a bit more in balance, but if you're craving lots of fruit, it will do just fine.

**Design** The filled-in "A"s are horrific, and don't get us started on the color scheme. Maybe it will deter drinkers and leave more for us...

# Aquinas Cabernet Sauvignon

**$15**

Don Sebastiani and Sons

**Style** Heavy New World red
**Country** USA (CA) **Vintage tasted** 2007
**Grapes** Cabernet Sauvignon
**Drink with** beef tenderloin, lamb tagine, mushroom soup
**Website** www.donandsons.com

Don Sebastiani adheres to a philosophy of consistency, in which vintage variations are reduced and a distinct brand character is preserved from year to year. While we vigorously disagree with that idea—we hold with the terroirists who believe that wine should be a reflection of the land and the season—we can't deny that this approach can still produce some thoroughly enjoyable wine. The task is made easier by the fact that Don Sebastiani is a negociant: rather than growing their own grapes, the winemakers buy grapes from different areas and blend them, enabling them to more easily adjust a wine's character.

**Nose** It has distinct vegetal aromas, as well as dense black fruit.

**Mouth** Our blind tasters had mixed feelings about the mouth, which they found very tannic and vegetal.

**Design** This one is just plain cool. The well spaced layout, great fonts, and simple colors exude hipness.

# Araucano Sauvignon Blanc

François Lurton

$13

**Style** Light New World white
**Country** Chile  **Vintage tasted** 2009
**Grapes** Sauvignon Blanc
**Drink with** grilled shrimp, soft cheeses
**Website** www.francoislurton.com

The Chilean Araucano brand is overseen by the French François Lurton, and this Sauvignon Blanc certainly bears his Old World mark. It's not as easily accessible as many New Zealand Sauv Blancs (it has vegetal, cabbage-y aromas rather than bright tropical fruit flavors), but if you're a true fan of the grape you'll love this wine.

**Nose** There's a powerful cabbage aroma, along with green apples and a whiff of that characteristic Sauv Blanc smell often compared to cat pee. Yum.

**Mouth** It definitely has an Old World vibe, with cooked green vegetables and a sort of chalkiness as the signature flavors.

**Design** It's a bit busy looking, but those strange-headed creatures are awfully adorable.

# Argento Bonarda

**Style** Heavy New World red
**Country** Argentina **Vintage tasted** 2008
**Grapes** Bonarda
**Drink with** a big old steak, fondly remembering your Malbec days
**Website** www.argentowine.com

Bonarda doesn't have much name recognition, possibly because it's so hard to pin down what the term refers to: there are several grapes in several countries that share the name. Argento's Bonarda is the same grape known in California as "Charbono," and it makes dense, rich, tannic wines perfect for hearty meat dishes. This bottle lives up to the grape's reputation, and our blind tasters were thrilled to discover a new alternative to Petite Sirah and hearty Cabs.

**Nose** Dark berries, mint, a hint of vegetable, and a meaty aroma—this aggressive nose is everything you'd want in a big New World red.

**Mouth** It's dry and tannic, with blackberries and chocolate to soften any harshness.

**Design** The silver leaf is a bit much, but given the name ("Argento" is the Latin world for "silver") it's tough to complain.

# Aria Estate Brut

Segura Viudas, Penedès DO

$12

**Style** Sparkling
**Country** Spain  **Vintage tasted** Non-Vintage
**Grapes** Macabeo, Parellada, Xarel-lo
**Drink with** hard cheeses, by itself
**Website** www.seguraviudasusa.com

Great values are coming out of Spain, and Cavas are some of the best: they're sold for a fraction of the price of their similarly made counterparts in Champagne. This bottle, the upscale cousin of last year's Segura Viudas winner, is fairly subtle for an inexpensive Cava. It refuses to hog the spotlight with intense acidity or bold flavors; instead, it goes for simplicity and food friendliness—something we definitely appreciate.

**Nose** Classic Cava apple mingles with an interesting mineral note—wonderful.

**Mouth** There's subtle apple that could afford to be a bit stronger—our blind tasters wanted a bit more acidity.

**Design** We can't sign onto the tacky name of the wine, and the silver shield is a bit much—for one thing, this label is so shiny it could be used as a sun signal. This is one of the Cavas least likely to fool your friends into thinking it's expensive.

# Aveleda Fonte Vinho Verde

*Three-time Wine Trials selection*

**$7**

**Style** Light Old World white
**Country** Portugal  **Vintage tasted** 2009
**Grapes** Arinto, Loureiro, Trajadura
**Drink with** sushi, gazpacho
**Website** www.aveleda.com

The ideal wine for cheap outdoor refreshment, Vinho Verde is meant to be drunk young: the word "verde" refers to the youthful greenness of the wine. The Fonte, crisp and lightly sparkling, is a perfect example of this classic style. It was last year's winner in the Light White category, and we'll even admit to having drunk it over ice on the occasional hot summer day.

**Nose** It's fairly faint, but lime and green apple are still recognizable. And really, you're not drinking this wine for the nose anyway.

**Mouth** Here's where the wine comes into its own: lots of acidity, apples, citrus, and that slight Vinho Verde prickle are why we love this wine so.

**Design** It's busy but harmonious, with an appropriately green bottle and a nostalgic and colorful label.

# Backsberg Chenin Blanc

**$12**

**Style** Aromatic New World white
**Country** South Africa  **Vintage tasted** 2008
**Grapes** Chenin Blanc
**Drink with** jalapeño poppers, chicken tacos
**Website** www.backsberg.com

Chenin Blanc is probably South Africa's signature white wine (it is also known there as "Steen"), and it is made in styles that range from decidedly sweet to bone-dry. This one is slightly off-dry, but with enough acid, clean citrus flavors, and bright minerality to avoid seeming sickly or cloying. Now that the World Cup is over, South Africa can at least take comfort in knowing they still have plenty of this stuff to go around.

**Nose** There's a mineral and slate quality that reminded one blind taster of Chablis. The aromas are wonderfully clean.

**Mouth** Refreshing flavors of citrus and stone dominate, aided by a strong dose of acidity that cleanses any lingering sugar.

**Design** It's unremarkable, but at least it's also inoffensive. And that dark green isn't bad at all.

# Banfi Centine Rosé

Toscana IGT

 **$13**

**Style** Rosé
**Country** Italy  **Vintage tasted** 2008
**Grapes** Sangiovese, Merlot, Cabernet Sauvignon
**Drink with** crab, fish stew
**Website** www.banfivintners.com

Go ahead, name a great Italian rosé widely available in the U.S. Give up? So had we, until our blind tasters found this gem from one of Tuscany's best-known producers. Made from Sangiovese, Merlot, and Cabernet Sauvignon—grapes that often make up the powerful red "Super Tuscans"—it's subtle and surprisingly refreshing. We're confident it will work equally well as a meal companion or a summery wine.

**Nose** Red fruit, a hint of earth, and a Champagne-like yeastiness make for a complex blend that kept our blind tasters coming back for more.

**Mouth** Despite the subtle fruit and yeastiness, it's crisp and refreshing.

**Design** It won't jump off a shelf at you, but that's okay. There's nothing wrong with speaking softly and carrying a big stick, now is there?

# Barefoot Bubbly Brut Cuvée

$10

**Style** Sparkling
**Country** USA (CA)  **Vintage tasted** Non-Vintage
**Grapes** Chardonnay
**Drink with** mimosas, by itself
**Website** www.barefootwine.com

We never would have predicted that two sparkling wines from this ubiquitous supermarket producer would have made the cut, but that's blind tasting for you. This bottle had a shocking amount of acidity for a budget wine, which usually tend to err on the sweet side. Some of our blind tasters even wondered if it had too much acidity, which almost never happens, so make sure you're in the mood for a tart, refreshing wine before you open this bottle.

**Nose** It has crisp mineral aromas and lots of apple.

**Mouth** As we said, the acidity was so intense that it made even our acid-happy tasters a bit nervous. It's also unusually bubbly, even for an inexpensive sparkling wine.

**Design** You can tell from a mile away that this is a budget sparkler, but that's not such a bad thing. There's something freeing about embracing your cheap-bubbly side.

# Barefoot Bubbly Extra Dry

$10

**Style** Sparkling
**Country** USA (CA)  **Vintage tasted** Non-Vintage
**Grapes** Chardonnay
**Drink with** finger food, guests you don't need to impress
**Website** www.barefootwine.com

Barefoot vies with Yellow Tail for the most-ubiquitous-mass-produced-wine-in-U.S.-stores award, but the folks there still manage to turn out some good wines. While "extra dry" normally designates sparklers that have a bit of noticeable sugar, this one has enough acidity to feel quite dry. It's extremely fizzy (probably past the point of naturalness), but somehow complaining about that seems like nitpicking.

**Nose** It's not terribly remarkable—few of our blind tasters had many specifics to offer—but it's crisp and lively, which is plenty at this price point.

**Mouth** The acid is impressive for an extra dry wine, and the foamy bubbles, while strange, are pleasant.

**Design** The shining foil and prominently displayed award are gaudy, but at least you'll never misplace the bottle.

# Barefoot Sauvignon Blanc

**Style** Light New World white
**Country** USA (CA)  **Vintage tasted** Non-Vintage
**Grapes** Sauvignon Blanc
**Drink with** sushi, softshell crab, mussels
**Website** www.barefootwine.com

To hear our blind tasters speak about this wine, you'd think they were discussing a pricey white Bordeaux rather than an inexpensive American Sauv Blanc from one of the most ubiquitous of producers. They were particularly taken with the minerality of this one—a term used to suggest that hard-to-define sense of wet rock after a rain or just to describe those "clean" qualities that clearly aren't fruit, earth, or vegetables (or animals—20 questions anyone?). Minerality is one of our favorite qualities in a white wine—finding it in a mass-produced, inexpensive wine is always exciting.

**Nose** It's minerally and nutty—not what we'd expect from this producer, but we're not complaining.

**Mouth** It's got nice acid (as a Sauv Blanc should), and it avoids the excesses of some New Zealand Sauv Blancs.

**Design** Why bother criticizing? Barefoot is interested in brand recognition, not style points.

# Belleruche Côtes-du-Rhône Blanc

M. Chapoutier

**Style** Light Old World white
**Country** France **Vintage tasted** 2008
**Grapes** Grenache Blanc, Clairette, Bourboulenc
**Drink with** goat cheese salad, fresh-caught fish
**Website** www.belleruchewines.com

Côtes-du-Rhône reds are increasingly popular these days with everyday drinkers, and if more whites like this start becoming widely available, we wouldn't be surprised if the whites catch on too. The grapes—Clairette and Bourboulenc, in particular—may be unfamiliar, but the delicate, fresh nose and clean acidity are old friends.

**Nose** Our blind tasters called it clean, fresh, and delicate, and they especially enjoyed the floral aromas.

**Mouth** Fresh acidity and bright citrus flavors wooed our blind tasters. This is a definite candidate for a good outdoor drink.

**Design** We like the clean, classic design—especially against the completely translucent bottle.

# Belleruche Côtes-du-Rhône Rosé

**$13**

M. Chapoutier

**Style** Rosé
**Country** France **Vintage tasted** 2008
**Grapes** Grenache, Cinsault, Syrah
**Drink with** Greek salad, itself
**Website** www.belleruchewines.com

M. Chapoutier has pulled a hat trick, managing to wow tasters with his white, red, and rosé, all in the same year. While we ultimately favor the lighter, more austere, and acidic Provence style of rosé, if you're a rosé novice, this might be a good point of entry without the cloying fruit of many New World rosés. Filled with red fruit, this one has a quality that prompted one of our blind tasters to call it "surprisingly wine-y." Of course all rosés are wines, but a rich berry flavor and full mouthfeel make this seem more like a light red wine than most.

**Nose** Our blind tasters were shocked at just how rich the red fruit was, but they certainly weren't complaining.

**Mouth** A bit of raspberry here, with some acid to liven things up; some of our tasters wished there were even more zip, though.

**Design** Yep, that label is still incredibly impressive. Do you think these guys give lessons?

# Belleruche Côtes-du-Rhône Rouge

M. Chapoutier

**Style** Heavy Old World red
**Country** France  **Vintage tasted** 2008
**Grapes** Syrah, Grenache
**Drink with** lamb tagine, burgers, blue cheese
**Website** www.belleruchewines.com

It's tough to find a Côtes-du-Rhône for under $15, much less one as delicious as this. Even more impressive, it's made by a vintner with seven generations of winemaking heritage. Côtes-du-Rhône is what made Syrah's reputation, before Australia and California got hold of it, and this bottle shows why. Balanced by the plusher, fruitier Grenache, the savory Syrah shows exactly why there's only one home for this grape.

**Nose** Herbs, smoke, sweaty animals, and pepper: just what we'd hope for in a Côtes-du-Rhône.

**Mouth** The Grenache is a bit more apparent here in the ripe berry flavors, but the herbs and tannins are coming mostly from the Syrah.

**Design** We don't think we've ever seen a wine bottle imprinted with Braille before, but it's a cool concept. And we have no objections to a vineyard crest when the vineyard has been around since the 19th century.

# Beringer Cabernet Sauvignon

**$11**

Founders' Estate • *Three-time Wine Trials selection*

**Style** Heavy New World red
**Country** USA (CA)  **Vintage tasted** 2007
**Grapes** Cabernet Sauvignon
**Drink with** roast beef, hard cheeses, lamb kebab
**Website** www.beringer.com

The folks at Beringer outdid themselves here…literally. In the initial *Wine Trials*, this $11 wine outscored their own $120 Beringer Private Reserve Cabernet. And the fact that this wine has been approved by our blind tasters every year since then just proves that its quality is no fluke. So hold on to your Benjamins—after all, he really was more of a beer guy.

**Nose** It's quite fruity (though not overripe), with inviting aromas of blackberry. There's also a smoky, meaty note to add complexity.

**Mouth** It's elegant and smooth, with flavors of fresh berries, dried fruit, mint, and smoke. No wonder it seems expensive.

**Design** We can't get on board with the big curly "B." But for $109 in savings, we can handle an ugly bottle.

# Big House Red

$8

**Style** Heavy New World red  **Country** USA (CA)
**Vintage tasted** 2009  **Grapes** Syrah, Petite Sirah, Grenache,
Montepulciano, Mourvèdre, Sangiovese, Aglianico, Tannat, Nero
D'Avola, Sargento, Touriga, Barbera, Petit Verdot
**Drink with** sloppy joes, by itself  **Website** www.bighousewine.com

Big House's website (complete with jailhouse animation) proudly
proclaims that the wine "lives up to that old fruit bomb moniker,"
and while that's true—this thing is packed with ripe fruit and
vanilla—it's still surprisingly balanced. And since it's packaged in a
box, the wine will keep for weeks once opened, rather than just a
day. We would consider keeping it in the fridge for frequent guilty
pleasure indulgences. Just don't tell the warden—it's contraband.

**Nose** It's rich, full of vanilla,
toast, and chocolate.

**Mouth** It certainly is big, with
bold fruit flavors—but
impressively balanced
nonetheless.

**Design** One of the sillier box
designs we've seen, with a
stylized cartoon of
cops-and-robbers shenanigans.
Still, these three-liter boxes are
bargains that are hard to beat.

# Big House White

**$8**

**Style** Aromatic New World white  **Country** USA (CA)
**Vintage tasted** 2009  **Grapes** Malvasia Bianca, Muscat Canelli,
Viognier, Grüner Veltliner, Pinot Gris, White Riesling
**Drink with** a bucket of ice, shrimp cocktail
**Website** www.bighousewine.com

This wine sent one of our blind tasters—an importer and wine
educator, no less—into fits of excitement; she insisted on taking the
rest of the box home. And we can certainly understand her
enthusiasm. The wine—not quite the laundry list of grapes that
make up the red version—consists of Malvasia Bianca, Muscat
Canelli, Grüner Veltliner, and several other underrated grapes. It's
intensely perfumed and sweet smelling, yet pleasingly dry. We'd
happily keep one of these three-liter boxes in the fridge for a late
afternoon treat.

**Nose** As we said, it's extremely
aromatic, with floral and citrus
notes.

**Mouth** Perfumed, big in the
mouth, and almost oily, it has just
enough acid to keep it from
seeming bloated or decadent.

**Design** Not a bad box. It doesn't
take itself too seriously, which
makes the wine inside that much
more impressive.

# Black Box Cabernet Sauvignon
*Three-time Wine Trials selection*

**Style** Heavy New World red  **Country** USA (CA)
**Vintage tasted** 2008  **Grapes** Cabernet Sauvignon,
Petite Sirah, Syrah, Merlot, Cabernet Franc, Petit Verdot
**Drink with** lamb stew, meatloaf
**Website** www.blackboxwines.com

Put your snobbery aside: boxed wine has many advantages, including larger volume and lower production costs, and vacuum sealed bags mean that you can keep the wine open for days or even weeks without significant loss of flavor. Still, we can't quite imagine keeping a big box of wine on the table for our next dinner party, especially one that looks like this. But we're working on it—the buzz is that box wines are the next big thing in the industry, so we'll have to adjust. And as this simple, fruity Cabernet shows, good wines can come in square packages.

**Nose** The ripe, almost cooked fruit and vegetal aromas were somewhat divisive, but many blind tasters did appreciate the hint of pepper.

**Mouth** It's quite soft, with lingering jammy fruit and more pepper.

**Design** Well, it's a big black box, so we have to give it credit for following through on the name. And one of these contains as much wine as four bottles, so here's to sustainability.

# Black Swan Shiraz

$8

**Style** Heavy New World red
**Country** Australia  **Vintage tasted** 2008
**Grapes** Shiraz
**Drink with** buffalo burgers, beef goulash
**Website** www.blackswanwine.com

Though distributed by the massive
E & J Gallo company and hailing
from Australia, the home of
massively overripe wines, this Shiraz
manages to be, if not subtle, at least
not unpleasantly over-the-top. It has
a hint of burnt rubber that can strike
many drinkers the wrong way, but
it's otherwise a rich, lovely wine. But
we must confess that we secretly
hope Australia will someday go back
to the Francophone "Syrah."

**Nose** That burnt rubber and
chemical note, while definitely there,
is offset by a lovely nose that seems
almost floral.

**Mouth** It's soft and round. One blind
taster called it lovely and delicate.

**Design** An Australian wine featuring
a cartooney critter? What a surprise.

# Bogle Cabernet Sauvignon

*Two-time Wine Trials selection*

**Style** Heavy New World red
**Country** USA (CA)  **Vintage tasted** 2008
**Grapes** Cabernet Sauvignon
**Drink with** chili, ribs
**Website** www.boglewinery.com

Last year, this wine and two other Bogle offerings were chosen by our blind tasters; this year Bogle managed another five stellar bottles. We have to admit we're impressed—they produce well over 100,000 cases of wine at a fairly low price point, and they do it well enough to wow our blind tasters. The Cab's rich, expansive New World flavors managed to wine over even the most skeptical of winos.

**Nose** Big, juicy aromas of raspberry and a note of spicy pepper come on pretty strong.

**Mouth** In marked contrast to its rich nose, the body is lean and tannic, with the distinct presence of oak.

**Design** These Bogle bottles are hefty, and their weight is a nice feature—one that often tricks people into thinking the wine is more expensive than it really is. The distressed look of the label adds a classy touch, too.

# Bogle Old Vine Zinfandel

*Three-time Wine Trials selection*

**Style** Heavy New World red
**Country** USA (CA)  **Vintage tasted** 2008
**Grapes** Zinfandel
**Drink with** game meats, spare ribs
**Website** www.boglewinery.com

Zinfandel is a pretty divisive grape; its manifestations can be too concentrated, fruity, and in-your-face for many drinkers. But if big, plush wines are your thing, the Bogle is a totally honest version (and has been for three years running). It's a classic California expression of the grape, with highly concentrated fruit, a touch of sweetness, and plenty of oak. But Bogle's Zin, at 14% alcohol, is very weak as far as New World incarnations of this grape go.

**Nose** It's got the big berry nose you'd expect (with lots of juicy black cherry), but there are also aromas of green pepper and even barnyard to add complexity.

**Mouth** It's definitely big, with a soft, round feel and a big juicy finish.

**Design** The subtly tapered Bogle bottle is a model of power and elegance. The creeping, almost primeval vine graphic and deep black background seem to echo the wine's qualities. This is one of our favorite bottles in the book.

# Bogle Petite Sirah

**Style** Heavy New World red
**Country** USA (CA)  **Vintage tasted** 2007
**Grapes** Petite Sirah
**Drink with** massive grilled steaks, aged cheeses
**Website** www.boglewinery.com

Misleading name aside, Petite Sirah is not a milder version of Syrah; in fact, they are two distinct grapes, and Petite Sirah is much bolder, more tannic, fruitier, and all-around bigger than its namesake. Bogle's version follows this pattern: big, juicy, and tannic, it's a perfect companion for a steak on a cold winter evening.

**Nose** Red berries dominate here, though our blind tasters differed on whether they were over the top. There's also a nice smoke note.

**Mouth** There's a strong blackberry flavor, as well as herbs. It's not as tannic as some Petite Sirahs (the tannins are still noticeable), and there's some nice acid thrown into the mix as well.

**Design** As always, Bogle leads the pack with its elegant bottle design.

# Bogle Pinot Noir
*Two-time Wine Trials selection*

**Style** Light New World red
**Country** USA (CA)  **Vintage tasted** 2008
**Grapes** Pinot Noir
**Drink with** herb-roasted chicken, Thanksgiving turkey
**Website** www.boglewinery.com

This Pinot is soft, filled with berries, and easy to love. Our blind tasters loved its simple, delicious flavors—which is all we'd ever ask from a New World Pinot at this price. And we must admit that we're often skeptical of California Pinots, as the heat and sunshine are enemies of this delicate grape. But this is a lovely version even though it's New World all the way. Best of all, its acidity will help it pair with a huge variety of your favorite foods.

**Nose** Our blind tasters called it "pretty," and enjoyed the rich red fruit.

**Mouth** It's soft, but its acidity provides structure and keeps it from being overdone.

**Design** The signature Bogle label looks nice on this well crafted bottle, but then again, most things would on such a pretty piece of glass.

# Bogle Sauvignon Blanc
*Two-time Wine Trials selection*

$9

WINNER

**Style** Light New World white
**Country** USA (CA)  **Vintage tasted** 2008
**Grapes** Sauvignon Blanc
**Drink with** lobster rolls, oysters, by itself
**Website** www.boglewinery.com

Last year it was Bogle's reds that made an impression on our blind tasters, but this year a white finally made its way into the top picks: this Sauvignon Blanc delivered enough tropical fruit and crisp acidity to deserve its share of the attention. There's certainly nothing subtle about this wine—and that's why many of our blind tasters loved it. Even a jaded drinker would have a hard time turning down its bold, refreshing flavors.

**Nose** Intense apple and tropical fruit aromas dominate. There's no mistaking that this is a Sauvignon Blanc.

**Mouth** More banana and other fruits here, along with bright acidity to counter what could otherwise be cloying flavors.

**Design** The effect of the Bogle taper is lessened by the wine's extremely pale color, which shows through the clear bottle. No design awards here, but it's inoffensive.

# Bohigas Crianza

**$15**

DO Catalunya

**Style** Light Old World red
**Country** Spain  **Vintage tasted** 2007
**Grapes** Tempranillo, Merlot, Cabernet Sauvignon
**Drink with** grilled vegetables, shish kebab
**Website** www.bohigas.es

As you've probably noticed, Cabernet Sauvignon is extremely popular. It's also easy to grow in a fairly wide range of climates, meaning that most wine countries produce some version of the grape—though quality can vary dramatically. It's always fascinating to see how the grape adapts to each country in which it's grown. The addition of it to this Spanish blend is a nice touch, giving a lovely balance of fruit, herbs, and earth.

**Nose** Our blind tasters found red and black fruit, herbs, and even a hint of cola.

**Mouth** Herbal and tannic, it borders on astringency without being unpleasant.

**Design** There's certainly nothing offensive here, and it's fine as a table wine. We reserve the more gushing praise for the bottle's contents.

# Bonterra Cabernet Sauvignon

$15

Mendocino County

**Style** Heavy New World red
**Country** USA (CA)  **Vintage tasted** 2007
**Grapes** Cabernet Sauvignon, Syrah, Petite Sirah, Merlot
**Drink with** venison, burgers
**Website** www.bonterra.com

Bonterra's grapes are "grown organically" but the wine is not "certified organic." This gets at the heart of a controversy in the wine world: to get organic certification, producers must jump through certain costly bureaucratic hoops, with the ironic results that certified organic wine is more likely than most to be mass-produced. Environmentally sustainable practices are much more important, so we applaud this producer for the growing methods—and for making this delicious Cabernet.

**Nose** It's distinctly New World in style, with flowers and black fruit that were either "yummy" or "overripe," depending on your taste.

**Mouth** This fruity, spicy mouth is full but not overpowering, showing impressive balance. One blind taster said it tasted expensive.

**Design** It looks quite elegant, with plenty of white space, well chosen fonts, and a simple, almost abstract sketch of a leaf.

# Borgo Magredo Extra Dry Prosecco  $15

**Style** Sparkling
**Country** Italy  **Vintage tasted** Non-Vintage
**Grapes** Prosecco
**Drink with** Chinese noodles, Thai salads
**Website** www.borgomagredo.com

Many ostensibly brut Proseccos have a strong touch of fruity sweetness to them, so you might think any extra dry version would be cloyingly sugary. Clearly, that's not the case: this wine is a bit sweet and certainly fruity, but it never loses its balance. It would be a great party wine and even better as an accompaniment to Thai, Vietnamese, and Chinese food.

**Nose** Sweet apples and a flowery aroma make a convincing case for this sparkler.

**Mouth** More of the same here. Though it's not a complex wine, it's no less delicious for that.

**Design** Maybe it's the color or the missed attempt at understated elegance, but there's something subtly off about this bottle.

# Brancott Sauvignon Blanc

Marlborough

**Style** Light New World white
**Country** New Zealand  **Vintage tasted** 2009
**Grapes** Sauvignon Blanc
**Drink with** vegetable tempura, lemon chicken
**Website** www.brancottvineyards.com

Brancott claims to have planted the first commercial vineyard in New Zealand's Marlborough region—no small distinction, as Marlborough produces a lot of the country's best Sauvignon Blancs. They also claim allegiance to sustainable agriculture, so you can feel good about drinking this wine. All in all, we're impressed, as were our blind tasters when they sampled this Sauvignon Blanc.

**Nose** It's definitely a New Zealand Sauv Blanc, with aggressive aromas of citrus, apples, and grass.

**Mouth** It's quite herbal—one blind taster compared it to asparagus in lemon juice. The acid is bracing, just the way we like it.

**Design** Understated and simple, this label has a nice color scheme, especially against the green of the bottle. But we're not fans of the faux-cursive font used for "Marlborough."

# Campo Viejo Rioja Reserva
*Two-time Wine Trials selection*

**Style** Light Old World red
**Country** Spain  **Vintage tasted** 2005
**Grapes** Tempranillo, Graciano, Mazuelo
**Drink with** chorizo, turkey
**Website** www.campoviejo.com

For the second year in a row, our blind tasters went crazy for this subtle, idiosyncratic wine. The winemakers at Campo Viejo have clearly resisted the trend for syrupy fruit bombs; instead, they concentrate on making balanced, food-friendly wine with some earthy character. We recommend that anyone who's never had a distinctly Old World wine try it—the flavors may not sound like something you'd want to taste, but we think you'll enjoy the experience.

**Nose** Dark, earthy aromas include underbrush, barnyard, and sour cherries.

**Mouth** The flavors of tea leaves, sour cherries, dirt, and smoke prompted one taster to call it "beautiful!".

**Design** The font's a bit cheesy, but we like the rich label color—it reminds us of the age and complexity of the wine.

# Çankaya
Kavaklidere

$11

**Style** Light Old World white
**Country** Turkey **Vintage tasted** 2008
**Grapes** Narince, Emir, Sultaniye
**Drink with** stuffed grape leaves, gazpacho
**Website** www.kavaklidere.com

Teaching Westerners to wrap their tongues around this tricky language is just the first challenge this Turkish winery faces. After that, it has to contend with the fact that its appellation is hardly a household name in elite wine circles (at least in modern times). Despite all that, they've managed to turn out this delicious table wine that's a textbook example of a fresh white. Oh, and by the way? Narince is pronounced "nah-REEN-jay." Good luck.

**Nose** It's very slightly aromatic, with a touch of fruit and a general sense of freshness.

**Mouth** With its impressive acidity, this one just feels refreshing. It's got an unexpected hint of yeastiness that we love.

**Design** It's nothing too exceptional. But we're so busy trying to decipher the language that it's tough to worry about layout.

# Casal Garcia Vinho Verde

*Three-time Wine Trials selection*

**Style** Light Old World white
**Country** Portugal  **Vintage tasted** Non-vintage
**Grapes** Trajadura, Loureiro, Arinto, Azal
**Drink with** ceviche, sushi, raw oysters
**Website** www.casalgarcia.com

One of a handful of wines to have appeared in all three editions of *The Wine Trials*, Casal Garcia continues to produce inexpensive, bright, summery wines. Don't be afraid to serve this bottle at a colder temperature than non-sparkling wines: the goal here is refreshment, not elaborate tasting notes. While Vinho Verde is technically not considered sparkling, there is a slight carbon-dioxide prickle. This allows it to pair easily with many different fresh, cold dishes—and could make it the sushi wine to end all.

**Nose** It's wonderfully clean, with citrus (mostly lemon and lime) dominating.

**Mouth** There's a slight fizz, a good pop of acidity, and bright citrus flavors; we'll bring a bottle next time we hit the beach.

**Design** The lace background and coat of arms are far too frilly, but the designers avoided the great-aunt's-house look through decent symmetry and harmony.

# Casal Garcia Vinho Verde Rosé

**\$8**

**Style** Rosé
**Country** Portugal  **Vintage tasted** Non-Vintage
**Grapes** Vinhão, Azal, Borracal
**Drink with** pollo en mole, salade Niçoise
**Website** www.casalgarcia.com

This year the Vinho Verde rosé from Casal Garcia joins its more traditional white wine cousin as a blind taster favorite. And while sparkling rosés can get a bad reputation (at least at lower price points), this wine suggests that that's an unfair stereotype: fuller and fruitier than a white, it's still just as dry, refreshing, and food friendly as any traditional Vinho Verde. We'd suggest using it to accompany slightly heftier dishes, or as a wonderful partner to fruit at a picnic.

**Nose** The raspberry and strawberry aromas, while intense, are balanced a bit by citrus.

**Mouth** That classic Vinho Verde prickle always makes us smile. It cuts the fruit here wonderfully, as does the acidity—though our acid-craving blind tasters suggested it could use even more on that front.

**Design** The pink of the wine certainly catches the eye; if they just got rid of a few lacey swirls, this could be a great label.

# Casillero del Diablo Cabernet Sauvignon

Concha y Toro

**Style** Heavy New World red
**Country** Chile  **Vintage tasted** 2008
**Grapes** Cabernet Sauvignon, Carménère
**Drink with** steak au poivre, beef Stroganoff
**Website** www.casillerodeldiablo.com

Concha y Toro is the big boy of Chilean winemaking, with more bottles than we can keep track of and a distribution network that boggles the mind. While quality can vary, they're perfectly capable of producing a good wine, as this bottle demonstrates. It tended to divide our blind tasters—you either love it or you hate it, apparently—but enough tasters loved it to include it among this year's selections.

**Nose** It's huge and intensely New World in style, with massive, jammy fruit, prune juice, and a hint of herbs.

**Mouth** Again, it's definitely big: big tannins, big alcoholic punch, big fruit flavors. You certainly don't have to worry about understatement.

**Design** They play up the Diablo theme without becoming hokey; we have to admit a guilty fondness for that shiny devil head just under the neck.

# Casteller Cava
*Two-time Wine Trials selection*

**$13**

**Style** Sparkling
**Country** Spain  **Vintage tasted** Non-Vintage
**Grapes** Macabeo, Parellada, Xarel-lo
**Drink with** pear and walnut salad, lightly seared fish

Cava, Spain's most famous bubbly, is the hot thing in the world of inexpensive sparkling wine. It's usually sharp and clean, with few of the yeasty or creamy flavors that define a good Champagne. That refreshing quality, along with impressive value, makes Cava the ideal summer bubbly for sipping on the porch with friends. For the second year in a row, Casteller's Cava is creamier and yeastier than most of its kin—a good transition wine for Champagne drinkers looking to find a sparkling wine they can drink without requiring a special occasion.

**Nose** Apples (a common Cava aroma), buttered toast, and an appealing yeastiness mingle here.

**Mouth** It's quite approachable, with acid that's not overwhelming and what seems to be a small touch of sweetness.

**Design** That castle reminds us of a chess rook, earning it an instant five brownie points. Well done—your move, Casteller.

# Casteller Cava Rosé

$10

**Style** Cava Rosé
**Country** Spain  **Vintage tasted** Non-Vintage
**Grapes** Trepat, Garnacha
**Drink with** chicken tacos, by itself

Our blind tasters' love affair with Spanish Cava continues with this rich, fruity rosé. And while many inexpensive rosé sparklers can be cloyingly sweet or nauseatingly jammy, this one retains enough of Cava's classic bite to be both well-balanced and accessible. It will also go well with a surprisingly large variety of foods—one taster reported an excellent dinner involving an upscale Mexican restaurant and a bottle of Casteller Rosé.

**Nose** It's not exactly complex: the aroma of strawberries dominates completely. But who complains about strawberry?

**Mouth** Strawberry continues to dominate. While some blind tasters thought it was a bit too sweet, most thought the acid/fruit/sugar balance was just about perfect.

**Design** The lone castle—Casteller is the Catalan word for castle-builder—is a model of simplicity and restraint. It does look a bit out of place, though, against all that pink.

# Cave de Lugny Mâcon-Villages

*Three-time Wine Trials selection*

**Style** Heavy Old World white
**Country** France  **Vintage tasted** 2008
**Grapes** Chardonnay
**Drink with** lobster bisque, Cobb salad
**Website** www.cave-lugny.com

Drinkers who have sworn off Chardonnay because of the heavy, over-oaked style of many Californian and Australian wines ought to take another look at white Burgundy. These wines are what first made Chardonnay's reputation, and they can reach stunning heights of quality—and, unfortunately, of price, too. Happily, the local village wines in Burgundy can be great values for those looking for a break from the California style: instead of rich, buttery textures and huge body, the wines produced by Cave de Lugny and its peers are clean, crisp, packed with minerality, and tingling with acidity.

**Nose** There's oak here, but it's restrained and balanced by a bright mineral aroma.

**Mouth** Continued minerality mingles with refreshing acidity.

**Design** It's a pretty run-of-the-mill white Burgundy bottle, outdated and vaguely evocative of a stuffy banquet in an awkward ballroom.

# Cerro Bercial
Bodega Sierra Norte

$11

FINALIST

**Style** Light Old World red
**Country** Spain **Vintage tasted** 2007
**Grapes** Tempranillo, Bobal
**Drink with** chorizo, seared lamb chops
**Website** www.bodegasierranorte.com

We're firm believers that Spain produces some of the best values in the wine world, and this bottle is great evidence. Emphasizing not just the more lauded Tempranillo but also Bobal, a grape that doesn't get much respect in the rest of Spain, Sierra Norte produces a wine that is as easy to like as it is to pair with food.

**Nose** It has a musty, Old World character, along with green pepper and red fruit.

**Mouth** Red fruit dominates here, accompanied by a hint of vanilla. And there's a great balance between acidity and tannins.

**Design** This bottle's all about utility. No bells, whistles, crests, or gilding here. But it seems that Sierra Norte has gone too far in this direction: we wouldn't be the least bit surprised to see this lying in a bleak $5-and-under bin somewhere. And we don't say that only because of the exaggerated dip on the "R" tail. Just mostly.

# Charamba Douro

*Two-time Wine Trials selection*

 **$8**

**Style** Light Old World red
**Country** Portugal  **Vintage tasted** 2007
**Grapes** Touriga Nacional, Touriga Franca, Tinta Barroca, Tinta Roriz
**Drink with** beef tenderloin, pasta alla puttanesca
**Website** www.aveleda.com

This two-time winner is yet more proof that Portugal is among the best countries in the world for wine value. Produced by Aveleda—responsible for quite a few *Wine Trials* winners in our three editions—this wine is made up of many of the same grape varieties that compose Port. Rather than being sweet, though, this wine is intensely dry and earthy. Why can't every red at this price point be as tasty and interesting?

**Nose** Our blind tasters identified manure and sour cherry, which smells better than it sounds.

**Mouth** There's tons of acidity—enough to prompt one taster to call it mouthwatering. There's also a nice spicy note that rounds out the flavors.

**Design** The wavy lines evoke hills, we suppose, but the font is silly safari-chic. Not our favorite bottle (though the wine inside makes up for any flaws).

# Château Damase
Bordeaux Supérieur

**Style** Heavy Old World red
**Country** France  **Vintage tasted** 2006
**Grapes** Merlot
**Drink with** roast chicken, pork chops, grilled vegetables

Though it comes from the obscure commune of Savignac in Bordeaux, this winery explicitly takes as its model the great Merlot-based wines of Saint-Émilion (of which Château Pétrus is the most famous example). Because the soil from the vineyards is made of clay, which is ideal for Merlot but inhospitable to Cabernet, the owner wisely decided to forgo the better known Cab-Merlot blend in favor of a pure Merlot wine. It has all the complexity of Bordeaux from better known areas, though it's still a bit rough around the edges.

**Nose** Merlot can be complex: black berries, green pepper, nutmeg, sweet spice, and barnyard aromas.

**Mouth** It's fruitier here, with decent tannins and fairly strong acidity.

**Design** With the exception of Château Mouton Rothschild, which hires famous artists to design its labels, most Bordeaux wineries have more or less the same bottle design: elegant script, sparse layout, and sketch of the winery. Check.

# Château La Gravière Blanc
## Entre-Deux-Mers

$8

**Style** Light Old World white
**Country** France  **Vintage tasted** 2009
**Grapes** Sauvignon Blanc, Sémillon
**Drink with** shrimp salad, chips and salsa

Like their red counterparts, the white wines of Bordeaux and Burgundy reflect two ends of a stylistic spectrum. In this case the comparison is between the rich, full Chardonnay of Burgundy and the leaner, tauter Sauvignon Blanc of Bordeaux. The contrast is not quite as sharp as it might at first seem, though: as is typical, Château La Gravière's white is a blend of the grassy, acidic Sauvignon Blanc and the fatter, almost oily Sémillon. It's one of the great blends in the wine world.

**Nose** The nose is so aromatic and fruity that our blind tasters thought this wine might hail from New Zealand. Among the aromas are grapefruit, passion fruit, lemon, and lime.

**Mouth** There's lots of fruit, along with a bit of vegetality, refreshing acidity, and a long citrus finish.

**Design** It fits the French mold with a lovely rendering of the château.

# Château Ste. Michelle Horse Heaven Sauvignon Blanc

**$15**

**Style** Light New World white
**Country** USA (WA)  **Vintage tasted** 2009
**Grapes** Sauvignon Blanc
**Drink with** TV dinners, chicken salad
**Website** www.ste-michelle.com

Château Ste. Michelle can't be blamed for the name (which evokes either a hokey summer camp or an equine graveyard) as Horse Heaven is Washington State's newest AVA. Thankfully, the wine itself is delicious enough to make us forget any issues we might have with the name. Refreshing and floral, it's just what we want in a domestic Sauvignon Blanc. Here's to dear old departed Trigger.

**Nose** It's powerful, with aromas of apple. Some blind tasters found it to be a bit stinky.

**Mouth** There are big orange notes, but there's enough acid to carry them through.

**Design** That central still life is beautiful, and wisely left with plenty of negative space surrounding it. Best of all, you hardly notice the signature (and terrible) font. Hallelujah.

# Château Ste. Michelle Sauvignon Blanc  $10

Columbia Valley • *Three-time Wine Trials selection*

**FINALIST**

**Style** Light New World white
**Country** USA (WA)  **Vintage tasted** 2009
**Grapes** Sauvignon Blanc
**Drink with** goat cheese salad, ceviche
**Website** www.ste-michelle.com

This Sauvignon Blanc is not as in-your-face as some of what you see coming out of New Zealand, and for that we like it. The style is a nice blend of Old World and New: the region's cool climate ensures that grapes aren't overripe or the wines too sweet. Château Ste. Michelle has consistently fared well with *Wine Trials* blind tasters and with the wine world at large; they seem to have mastered the art of producing delicious, interesting wines for the budget drinker.

**Nose** The aromas are very, very faint. Blind tasters definitely knew this was a Sauvignon Blanc, and there was a hint of florality, too.

**Mouth** It's silky and rich, with plenty of floral notes, lemon-lime hints, and lots of good acidity.

**Design** It's got that classic Château Ste. Michelle look: trying to be classy, but ending up old and stilted, largely because of the cursive font.

# Château Ste. Michelle Syrah
Columbia Valley

$13

**Style** Heavy New World red
**Country** USA (WA)  **Vintage tasted** 2006
**Grapes** Syrah, Mourvèdre, Viognier
**Drink with** rabbit stew, pot roast
**Website** www.ste-michelle.com

Syrah is an impressively versatile grape: herbal and animal in southern France, massive and jammy under the alias "Shiraz" in Australia, it's capable of remarkably different expressions depending on where and how it's grown. Château Ste. Michelle walks a nice balance between fruit and elegance: it's sleek and never jammy, but there's still plenty of rich berry flavor for an American palate. Once again, Ste. Michelle has found the sweet spot that we'd love to see more American producers emulate.

**Nose** There's rich blackberry and a not-unpleasant aroma one blind taster compared to sawdust.

**Mouth** Silky and rich, it has black fruit and a touch of vanilla.

**Design** We're never fans of that awful cursive script—but we only criticize out of love. And on the bright side, the Burgundy bottle shape, unusual for Ste. Michelle, is impressively elegant.

# Columbia Crest Grand Estates Cabernet

Columbia Valley

**Style** Heavy New World red
**Country** USA (WA)  **Vintage tasted** 2007
**Grapes** Cabernet Sauvignon, Merlot, Cabernet Franc, Syrah
**Drink with** skirt steak, venison
**Website** www.columbiacrest.com

Columbia Crest is Washington State's mass-market powerhouse (and a perennial *Wine Trials* favorite), with a portfolio that includes four different lines of wines. This year three wines made the cut—two from the lower-priced Two Vines brand, plus this Cab from the slightly pricier Grand Estates portfolio. While Grand Estates wines have been overbearing in the past, this bottle hits a great spot between rich flavors and restraint.

**Nose** Ripe fruit, eucalyptus, earth, and green pepper were all hits with our blind tasters.

**Mouth** There's dark fruit here, along with chocolate and definite evidence of oak.

**Design** It looks like a standard American mid-range Cabernet bottle, which isn't bad at all. We're a bit tired of the vineyard sketch motif, though.

# Columbia Crest Two Vines Riesling

$8

FINALIST

*Two-time Wine Trials selection*

**Style** Aromatic New World white
**Country** USA (WA) **Vintage tasted** 2008
**Grapes** Riesling
**Drink with** oysters, aged cheese (not together)
**Website** www.columbiacrest.com

Unlike many New World Rieslings, which can be insipid or cloying, this wine is light, refreshing, and just plain fun to drink. As is the case with many good Rieslings, it walks a delicate tightrope between sweetness and acidity. We'll happily drink this bottle outside, or as a complement to anything from Thai food to shellfish.

**Nose** It's not particularly fruity; instead our blind tasters detected honey, brine, and a slight vegetality.

**Mouth** There's fruit here, along with great mouthwatering acidity. Just what we look for in a budget domestic Riesling.

**Design** Compared to the other labels in the Columbia Crest Portfolio, this design is a work of art. The sleek bottle, elegant glass, and well-chosen color scheme showcase the wine perfectly.

# Columbia Crest Vineyard 10

**Style** Aromatic New World white
**Country** USA (WA)  **Vintage tasted** 2008
**Grapes** Chardonnay, Sauvignon Blanc, Sémillon
**Drink with** fruits of the sea, white fish, by itself
**Website** www.columbiacrest.com

In the constant quest for *more* in wine (more acid, more tannins, more fruit, etc.), it's easy to overlook the value of a simple white wine that pleases rather than overwhelms. Vineyard 10 is exactly that wine, with restrained, almost faint aromas and flavors that are pleasant and clean. For geekier drinkers, the grape mix is interesting: it's not often you find Chardonnay, Sauvignon Blanc, Sémillon, and unnamed other varieties in the same bottle. Whether you're looking for something light enough to pair with simple white fish or just a porch-sipper, this wine should hit the spot.

**Nose** It's extremely light, with mainly floral aromas.

**Mouth** Our blind tasters described it as clean, floral, and grassy and compared it to fresh air.

**Design** The color scheme makes us a bit queasy, but the bottle shape and well designed label do their job perfectly.

# Concannon Petite Sirah
Limited Release • *Three-time Wine Trials selection*

**Style** Heavy New World red
**Country** USA (CA)  **Vintage tasted** 2007
**Grapes** Petite Sirah, Petit Verdot
**Drink with** lamb stew, meat pies, carne asada
**Website** www.concannonvineyard.com

Concannon built its reputation on Petite Sirah, and the folks there claim to have produced the world's first single-varietal version. Their skill at turning out dense, luscious Petite Sirah—with flavors and aromas that wouldn't be out of place in $30 or $40 bottles of wine—certainly bolsters their claim. If you're a fan of bold, powerful New World reds that aren't sweet or jammy (a specialty of good Petite Sirah), this bottle should hit the spot.

**Nose** It's full of black fruit, pepper, and what one blind taster described as compost.

**Mouth** Loads of tannins, rich black fruit, and a huge, round mouthfeel combine to form a wine that can only be described as a blast.

**Design** We find the raised graphic fascinating. While the bottom of the tree is tight and controlled, the branches transform into a semi-abstract splatter straight out of Jackson Pollock's portfolio.

# Condes de Albarei Albariño

($12)

DO Rias Baixas

**Style** Light Old World white
**Country** Spain  **Vintage tasted** 2009
**Grapes** Albariño
**Drink with** sushi, sautéed white fish, lemon roasted chicken
**Website** www.condesdealbarei.com

Based on our recent encounters at restaurants and wine stores, Spanish Albariño seems to be coming into its own. We couldn't be happier. This grape (known as Alvarinho across the Portuguese border) makes wonderfully fresh food wines that we'll happily drink with a huge variety of dishes. This bottle is especially aromatic and fruity, which will help its crowd appeal, yet it retains impressive acid and freshness.

**Nose** Tropical fruit, oranges, roses, peach, and apricot combine to form a lively nose.

**Mouth** The same fruity and floral flavors continue, joined by bright acidity that keeps the wine from seeming cloying and helps it pair with food.

**Design** The mix of fonts is distracting and busy. What's more, they aren't even using great specimens to start with. We expect more from the stylish Spanish.

# Cono Sur Bicycle Cabernet Sauvignon

Central Valley

**Style** Heavy New World red
**Country** Chile  **Vintage tasted** 2008
**Grapes** Cabernet Sauvignon
**Drink with** roast lamb, steak, onion soup
**Website** www.conosur.com

We're always suckers for a good pun (if you haven't picked up on it, say the name of this wine three times fast), so we were delighted when the brown paper bag came off this Chilean bottle. Furthermore, the winery claims that the bicycle represents its commitment to the environment—a commitment that extends to using bikes rather than motor vehicles to travel across and between the vineyards. That's an idea to which we're happy to raise a glass.

**Nose** It has berries, green bell pepper, and a hint of soft vanilla. Impressively complex.

**Mouth** Along with the berries you'd expect, there's a smoky green pepper flavor and a distinct leather note.

**Design** We like the bike much better than yet another cuddly animal, and we're fans of the minimalist design.

# Cortijo Rioja

*Two-time Wine Trials selection*

**Style** Light Old World red
**Country** Spain  **Vintage tasted** 2009
**Grapes** Tempranillo, Garnacha
**Drink with** beef carpaccio, spare ribs
**Website** www.aldeanueva.com

Today's Riojas are capable of being earthy, barnyardy, thoroughly traditional wines, or aggressively cherry-flavored and jammy. Unlike last year's fruit-forward effort, this one occupies a nice middle ground, with intense fruit flavors balanced by darker, richer undertones. It's a nice transition for New World drinkers trying to gain an appreciation for the less accessible Old World style, as well as a great example of the range and versatility of the Rioja region.

**Nose** It has "crazy cherry," according to one blind taster, as well as an earthy, almost muddy aroma.

**Mouth** More fruit here (so rich that it's bordering on jammy), along with herbaceous flavors and some green pepper.

**Design** Simple and understated, the design is Spanish hip, right down to the intentionally childlike rendering of the house. And we love the burnt orange color.

# Cycles Gladiator Pinot Grigio

$10

**Style** Light New World white
**Country** USA (CA)  **Vintage tasted** 2009
**Grapes** Pinot Grigio, Muscat
**Drink with** prosciutto and melon, clams
**Website** www.cyclesgladiator.com

There aren't many wines that can say they've been banned in the state of Alabama. After Cycles' label was deemed pornographic in the state, the winery did the only logical thing it could: it sold T-shirts. The shirts, which featured a crossed-out copy of the label and the catchy tag line "taste what they're missing," are surprisingly stylish. We might order a few as collectors' items.

**Nose** It's fairly complex for a Pinot Grigio: tropical fruit, citrus, and flowers all make an appearance.

**Mouth** Some spice, tropical fruit, apples, and a decent hit of acid round out the wine.

**Design** Original prints of this evocative 19th-century French bicycle-ad drawing go for as much as $50,000. We wouldn't pay that much, but we do love the artwork.

# Cycles Gladiator Pinot Noir

$14

**Style** Light New World red
**Country** USA (CA)  **Vintage tasted** 2008
**Grapes** Pinot Noir
**Drink with** pulled pork, barbecue sandwiches
**Website** www.cyclesgladiator.com

This is a perfect Pinot Noir for non-Pinot drinkers. Plush and fruity, this wine has none of the earthiness or thinness that can make European Pinot Noir such a challenge to people who grew up with and still favor fruity New World wines. One blind taster called it simply "yummy," and we'd have a hard time disagreeing.

**Nose** It's mostly red fruit here, though there's a slight vegetal aroma as well.

**Mouth** Round and easy to like, it's wonderfully approachable.

**Design** The Francophile Burgundy bottle holds no hint of the extreme New World character of the wine. Still, it's fun and escapist. If weirdo labels are moving in this direction and away from stuffable animals and irrelevant curse words, then we're all for it.

# Dancing Bull Cabernet Sauvignon

$12

*Two-time Wine Trials selection*

**Style** Heavy New World red
**Country** USA (CA) **Vintage tasted** 2007
**Grapes** Cabernet Sauvignon
**Drink with** roasted vegetables, beef stew
**Website** www.dancingbullwines.com

Where last year's Dancing Bull was packed full of berries and fruit, this one shows the other side of Cabernet: dense and vegetal, it's an excellent food wine. We also recommend checking out the Dancing Bull website, which is so complex and filled with unexpected features that we felt like we were playing a video game. We can only imagine how cheap this wine would be if the producer didn't have to pay for web development.

**Nose** It's very green, with the smell of tomato vines and other growing things. There's also a hint of clove in there.

**Mouth** There are still vegetables here, but spice takes over. It even reminded one blind taster of Christmas potpourri.

**Design** It's technically a critter wine, but the rich red background and silhouetted bull won us over. Producers really need to cut down on the red-and-gold motif, though.

# Diflora Chianti 365
Chianti DOCG

**$7**

**BARGAIN**

**Style** Light Old World red
**Country** Italy  **Vintage tasted** 2007
**Grapes** Sangiovese
**Drink with** spaghetti and meatballs, pizza

This is definitely one of the cheaper Chiantis out there, and it was also one of our blind tasters' favorites. It's more fruity than many of our other Chianti selections, but no less likeable for that. And at this price, we'd be happy to have it as a table wine with any Italian meal.

**Nose** It's intensely fruity, with berry and cherry aromas.

**Mouth** Big and juicy, it maintains its cherry appeal. There's a slight hit of tannin at the end, but it's much less acidic than many Chiantis.

**Design** This might be one of the very ugliest bottles in the whole book. It's busy yet manages to convey nothing. The small caps are no good, and what is with the capitalization of the last letter of the word "Chianti"? It makes us think of idiotic Vegas Italianate design. The color is off-putting, and the 365 logo doesn't go with the rest. In sum, it's abhorrent.

# Domaine Les Salices Viognier

$12

Condrieu

**Style** Aromatic Old World white
**Country** France  **Vintage tasted** 2008
**Grapes** Viognier
**Drink with** Thai curries, jerk chicken
**Website** www.francoislurton.com

Viognier makes some of the roundest, most aromatic wines around. In the French Condrieu (in northern Rhône) it can be stunningly rich and delicious, and it's been steadily catching on as a New World grape as well. It's not to everyone's taste (one of our blind tasters compares it to old lady perfume), but for most people it's easy to like. This one is a classic example, with rich floral aromas that should please the crowds.

**Nose** It lives up to its reputation, with roses, orange, fruit, and flowers.

**Mouth** More of the same here; it's impressive how balanced it manages to be. One blind taster thought it might have just been a well done Chardonnay.

**Design** It's simple and classic, though the "limited edition" notice needs to go: that froofy script is awful, and there's no such thing as limited edition for a $12 wine with tens of thousands of bottles.

## Domaine Ste. Michelle Blanc de Noirs

**$12**

**Style** Sparkling
**Country** USA (WA)  **Vintage tasted** Non-Vintage
**Grapes** Pinot Noir
**Drink with** seafood paella, frittata
**Website** www.domaine-ste-michelle.com

Blanc de Noirs Champagnes (or, in this case, sparkling wines) earn their name because they are composed exclusively of Pinot Noir, a classic red wine grape. This tends to give them a fruitier, richer profile than wines made from the traditional blend of Chardonnay, Pinot Noir, and Pinot Meunier. This bottle isn't as stereotypically Pinot Noir-ish as some Blanc de Noirs, but there's certainly that hint of extra richness that appealed powerfully to our tasters.

**Nose** Our blind tasters found raisins, apples, crackers, citrus, and that Champagne yeast aroma.

**Mouth** There's tons of apple flavor here, along with impressive acid. We could drink this all day.

**Design** The gold leaf seems unnecessarily gaudy—why can't the bottle be as simple and appealing as the wine? Give us back the old Domaine Ste. Michelle bottles, which were less frilly and classier.

# Domaine Ste. Michelle Brut

Cuvée • *Three-time Wine Trials selection*

**Style** Sparkling
**Country** USA (WA) **Vintage tasted** Non-Vintage
**Grapes** Chardonnay, Pinot Noir
**Drink with** special occasions, Chinese food
**Website** www.domaine-ste-michelle.com

A perennial *Wine Trials* favorite, Domaine Ste. Michelle beat the competition for the third year running in this year's blind tastings. Why? Well, it's made in the traditional method of Champagne, and the grapes are from Washington's Columbia Valley, whose climate is similar to that of the Champagne region in France. However, the style is fresher, lighter, and more approachable than Champagne. Best of all, you're not paying for millions of dollars in glossy magazine ads featuring scantily clad supermodels.

**Nose** Most of our blind tasters commented on the unmistakable scent of crisp apples, with some even comparing it to apple pie.

**Mouth** The wine is delicate and balanced, with plenty of acidity and refreshing carbonation to counter the lush apple taste.

**Design** The bottle's trying to look expensive, but you know better.

# Domäne Wachau Grüner Veltliner

Federspiel Terrassen • *Two-time Wine Trials selection*

**Style** Light Old World white
**Country** Austria  **Vintage tasted** 2008
**Grapes** Grüner Veltliner
**Drink with** fried fish, clams
**Website** www.domaene-wachau.at

Located in Austria's beautiful Wachau Valley and overlooking the Danube, Domäne Wachau occupies an enviable piece of land. The wines coming from this producer are wonderful, serving as fitting ambassadors for their still somewhat unknown region. Since last year, when the previous vintage of this wine was a *Wine Trials* selection, Grüner Veltliner has made significant strides in popularity: while it's been a favorite of wine geeks for years, the grape is now appearing on down-scale restaurant wine lists and corner liquor stores.

**Nose** It's faint—one could say delicate—and floral, with a layer of citrus underneath.

**Mouth** A subtle melon flavor works well with the wine's near-effervescence and crisp acidity.

**Design** A very grown-up label for a very grown-up wine coming from a very grown-up producer. The lack of frills is what Grüner Veltliner is all about.

# Doña Paula Los Cardos Malbec
Mendoza

**Style** Heavy New World red
**Country** Argentina  **Vintage tasted** 2008
**Grapes** Malbec
**Drink with** shish kebab, potatoes au gratin
**Website** www.donapaula.com

Malbec is all the rage these days among casual drinkers, and it's easy to see why—this wine is nothing if not likeable. Reliable bargains and decent at pairing with most meats, these wines have plenty of New World fruit without the worst excesses of Australian Shiraz and its kin. Los Cardos' effort lives up to the grape's reputation, delivering ripe berries and chocolate with an easygoing mouthfeel.

**Nose** Our blind tasters picked out cherry, chocolate, and pepper.

**Mouth** It's fairly complex for such an easy-drinking wine, with a bit of pleasant sourness and even more fruit.

**Design** It's clean and well thought out, with a sensible screwtop. We approve.

# Dr. L Riesling
Loosen Brothers

**Style** Aromatic Old World white
**Country** Germany **Vintage tasted** 2008
**Grapes** Riesling
**Drink with** Thai curries, jerk chicken
**Website** www.drloosen.com

WINE OF THE YEAR

$12 WINNER

Dr. Loosen is one of the most expensive German Riesling producers, regularly overpricing bottles into the hundreds of dollars. Loosen's value wine, though, is fresh, balanced, and utterly delicious, even though it has less minerality than many of his prestige wines. This bottle should be an easy introduction to German Riesling for the uninitiated.

**Nose** Our blind tasters loved the complex nose, with its honey, apricot, apple, and a clean metallic scent.

**Mouth** This wine achieves the classic German balance of honeyed sweetness with zingy, refreshing acidity that leaves your mouth clean and ready for another sip.

**Design** This logo is frilly and not cool at all. Why can't this bottle bear a label that's as clean and classic as the wine inside?

# Eder Rioja
Bodegas Valdelana

**Style** Light Old World red
**Country** Spain  **Vintage tasted** 2009
**Grapes** Tempranillo, Viura
**Drink with** grilled pork chops, bratwurst
**Website** www.bodegasvaldelana.com

Tempranillo is to Spain what Sangiovese or Nebbiolo are to Italy: famous national grape varieties capable of producing earthy, sophisticated, age-worthy wines. Tempranillo forms the core of the wonderful wines of Rioja, as well as those of Ribera del Duero. But unlike those wines, which are often aged for many years before being released to the public, this junior Rioja is young and fresh. So if you've ever wondered what that Rioja might have tasted like soon after it first fermented, this should give you a clue.

**Nose** Lots of cherry, along with some sawdust and green, grassy aromas.

**Mouth** More fruit here. Bold tannins should help it stand up to fairly hefty meat dishes.

**Design** The script name is so ornate that it looks like Arabic calligraphy. Paired with the simplicity of the rest of the bottle, it looks exceptionally classy. Put it on the dinner party list.

# El Albar Barricas

François Lurton, DO Toro

$13

**Style** Light Old World red
**Country** Spain  **Vintage tasted** 2008
**Grapes** Tinta de Toro
**Drink with** fried chicken, lamb sausage
**Website** www.francoislurton.com

Frenchman François Lurton must get some raised eyebrows in proud Spanish wine country. But there's no need for nationalism: though Lurton seems to be in nearly every major wine country in the world, many of his bottles are shockingly delicious. Even more impressive, they tend to reflect the characteristics of grape, soil, and national traditions rather than one winemaker's personal style. This one, for instance, has the meaty, herbal, Old World flavors that we love in Spanish wines, along with a crowd-pleasing burst of fruit.

**Nose** Dense sour cherries, vegetal aromas, and a yeasty note rule here.

**Mouth** The basic taste known as umami in Japanese is a definite player. Otherwise the wine is herbal and vegetal, with food-friendly acid and tannin.

**Design** The attempt to look ancient actually works, for once. With its medieval script and lack of distracting pictures, this bottle exudes Old World class.

# El Coto Rioja Crianza
DOC • *Two-time Wine Trials selection*

**Style** Light Old World red
**Country** Spain  **Vintage tasted** 2006
**Grapes** Tempranillo
**Drink with** turkey, hearty soups
**Website** www.elcoto.com

A relatively young winery (it was founded in the early 1970's), El Coto turns out Riojas that are positively ancient in style. Dusty and leathery, both this year's and last year's offerings were packed with the sour cherries and rustic aromas that are part of the classic Rioja profile. We love it, but then, we're suckers for the Old World. If you've never had an old-school Spanish wine, we suggest you at least give it a try—retro's in, after all.

**Nose** It's earthy, with plenty of red fruit to round out the rough edges.

**Mouth** It's silky in the mouth, with a wonderfully long, earthy finish.

**Design** The bottle looks even more ancient than the wine tastes. If the producers would just lose the elk and the crest, it wouldn't be half bad—and besides, no winery founded in the '70s should have a crest in the first place.

# Estancia Riesling

Monterey County

**Style** Aromatic New World white
**Country** USA (CA)  **Vintage tasted** 2008
**Grapes** Riesling, Chardonnay
**Drink with** pork sausage, roast chicken
**Website** www.estanciaestates.com

Our blind tasters were shocked to learn that this wine was domestic: with its bright minerality, clean aromas, and characteristic "petrol" scent (trust us, it's a good thing), this bottle could easily be mistaken for a German Riesling. With only a hint of sugar and abundant acidity, this food-friendly wine feels almost dry—and it will go well with everything from pork to East Asian cuisine.

**Nose** Most of our tasters commented on the wine's minerality—a term that's hard to define but easy to recognize. Think wet rock after a rainstorm. There are flowers and fruit here too.

**Mouth** Words like "restrained" and "lovely" kept cropping up in our blind tasters' notes.

**Design** There's something about the bottle that reminds us of summer days. It also doesn't have the classic Riesling shape (thinner, German style) and instead looks more like a Burgundy bottle.

# Fonseca Twin Vines Vinho Verde

*Two-time Wine Trials selection*

**Style** Light Old World white
**Country** Portugal  **Vintage tasted** 2009
**Grapes** Loureiro, Trajadura, Pedernã, Alvarinho
**Drink with** cold crab, chicken salad
**Website** www.jmftwinvines.com

With its pleasing fruit and citrus flavors, mouthwatering acidity, and shockingly low price tag, it's a mystery why Vinho Verde isn't served on every porch in America. Whatever the reason, we're happy to see that these Portuguese wines are slowly catching on—with this being the latest of many fantastic examples in this book alone. Fonseca's is a perfect example of the classic Vinho Verde style, though there's more of a floral component to this wine than many others have. Either way, we'd happily drink it with shellfish or as a party wine.

**Nose** There's intense floral, apple, and citrus. One blind taster said that the smell made his mouth water.

**Mouth** There's crisp citrus here, with that classic Vinho Verde prickle from the slight effervescence.

**Design** "Busy" doesn't begin to describe what's going on here. The color scheme is nice, but the exploding tangle of vines looks like it's in need of some serious pruning.

# Foxhorn Chardonnay

**$6**

**BARGAIN**

**Style** Heavy New World white
**Country** USA (CA)  **Vintage tasted** Non-Vintage
**Grapes** Chardonnay
**Drink with** salmon, creamy chicken dishes
**Website** www.foxhornwinery.com

Well, you won't be winning any style points for drinking this one. Our blind tasters—who almost universally loved it—were shocked to find that this wine came in a jug. And not a tasteful jug, either: the kind of tacky jug that normally contains undrinkable plonk. This California Chard, though, was anything but tacky. Refreshing, bright with citrus, and with just enough oak to make it juicy, this is a wine we'll happily close our eyes and pour. Or put it right back in its brown paper bag.

**Nose** Our tasters loved the clean, fresh nose, with its plentiful fruit.

**Mouth** Even our most oak-averse tasters had no problems here, and they even admired the "good juicy mouthful" and hint of vanilla perfectly balanced by citrus.

**Design** Um, we recommend pouring it in the kitchen—there's no need for guests to see this monstrosity.

# Freixenet Carta Nevada Brut

**Style** Sparkling
**Country** Spain  **Vintage tasted** Non-Vintage
**Grapes** Xarel-lo, Macabeo, Parellada
**Drink with** sushi, mild curries
**Website** www.freixenet.com

Freixenet is a familiar face in *The Wine Trials*, but typically it's their Cordon Negro line that makes the cut. But the Carta Nevada wines made a great showing this year, along with their black-bottled cousins. The wines have a deliciously funky, Champagney nose. This one, with its complex flavors and reasonable price tag, would be a perfect bottle to explore with various food pairings. That's right: you can actually drink Cava with food, not just toast to big bonuses and hose down models.

**Nose** It has an interesting blend of clean, mineral aromas, citrus, and a funkier cheeselike aroma that's reminiscent of Champagne.

**Mouth** Cheese, apple, and plenty of acid.

**Design** We like the metallic foil and relatively simple label, but the color of the bottle is off-putting (a bit like urine, in fact) and susceptible to light contamination.

# Freixenet Cordon Negro Brut

*Three-time Wine Trials selection*

**$12**

**Style** Sparkling
**Country** Spain  **Vintage tasted** Non-Vintage
**Grapes** Parellada, Macabeo, Xarel-lo
**Drink with** fresh strawberries, brunch, by itself
**Website** www.freixenet.com

Unsurprisingly, given the freedom of sparkling wines to mix vintages, our *Wine Trials* bubblies have remained consistent year to year. For the third year in a row, this wine impressed our blind tasters with mouthwatering acidity and enticing aromas. And don't worry—despite Freixenet's relentless advertising featuring dangerously attractive people partying with celebrities, there's no rule against frumpy or non-celebratory drinkers. Which is good, because we enjoy this one anytime.

**Nose** It's intensely aromatic, with citrus, apples, and flowers.

**Mouth** The acid is bracing and definitely intense enough to allow this sparkler to pair with food.

**Design** The extremely dark Freixenet bottle mysteriously conceals its contents. Some drinkers probably buy it out of sheer curiosity.

# Freixenet Cordon Negro Extra Dry $10

*Three-time Wine Trials selection*

**Style** Sparkling
**Country** Spain  **Vintage tasted** Non-Vintage
**Grapes** Parellada, Macabeo, Xarel-lo
**Drink with** huevos rancheros, fruit salad
**Website** www.freixenet.com

Know how to pronounce Freixenet? Well, with three wines in this year's *Wine Trials* and two in the last, it's worth learning: "Fresh-eh-net" (the word is Catalan). This wine may be Spanish, but for the second year in a row our blind tasters mistook it for a Champagne—its toastiness, yeastiness, and funky aromas are distinctly French. It's worth trying it with slightly spicy foods, as the sweetness creates a nice balance and soothes the mouth.

**Nose** It's stinky and yeasty, with the sharp green apple that is a Cava trademark.

**Mouth** As usual with extra dry sparkling wines, there's some sweetness here. But the balance is impressive, especially for this price.

**Design** There's a lot to be said for the black bottle, although it has one major fault: it's tough to see how much wine is left. We suggest just drinking it all.

# Fumées Blanches

**$11**

François Lurton

**Style** Light Old World white
**Country** France  **Vintage tasted** 2009
**Grapes** Sauvignon Blanc
**Drink with** fresh mozzarella, Greek salad, pasta salad
**Website** www.francoislurton.com

You might not know it by the exorbitant prices of Bordeaux, Burgundy, and Champagne, but France can be an impressive country for value wine. Lesser-known regions such as the Languedoc can rival even Spain and Portugal in quality-to-price ratio. This Sauvignon Blanc (Fumé Blanc is an alternate name for the grape), comes from Gers, an obscure region in the southwest of France. It's a great example of how exciting these as-yet-relatively-unknown regions can be.

**Nose** With a nice balance between vegetal, floral, grassy, and fruit (especially melon) aromas, this wine has something for everyone.

**Mouth** More of the same here, along with an acidity that's refreshing but not overpowering. This would be an ideal summer sipper.

**Design** The subtle mountainscape and woven lowercase serif fonts are models of understated elegance. Well done.

# Fuzelo Vinho Verde
*Two-time Wine Trials selection*

**Style** Light Old World white
**Country** Portugal  **Vintage tasted** 2009
**Grapes** Alvarinho, Trajadura
**Drink with** raw oysters, ceviche

Vinho Verde is all about biting acidity and that slight effervescent prickle, and this two-time *Wine Trials* selection has plenty of both. High acidity can be an acquired taste, but once you've caught the bug it's like being a roller-coaster fanatic: the bigger the better. Meant for sipping outside on a too-hot summer day, this wine will also fare well with sushi—and its lemon-lime flavors make it a natural fit for ceviche. The acidity might strip the enamel off your teeth, but at least you'll have a great time.

**Nose** It's wonderfully clean, full of the smell of stone and citrus.

**Mouth** It's more about the texture and biting acidity than the flavor (though the stone and citrus is still here).

**Design** It looks like a flower child vomited up this label design. Still, you can't accuse them of being unnecessarily subtle.

# Gabbiano Chianti Classico

Chianti DOCG

**FINALIST**

**$12**

**Style** Light Old World red
**Country** Italy  **Vintage tasted** 2007
**Grapes** Sangiovese
**Drink with** pasta with red sauce, roast chicken
**Website** www.gabbiano.com

After an unfortunate period in the '70s, when the wicker baskets that held the wine were given more attention than the liquid itself and Chianti became known as Italian for "undrinkable," this delicious red's reputation has fully recovered—or deserves to, anyway. This quintessential food wine is one of our go-to choices for tomato sauces, game meats, and a host of other Italian dishes. Gabbiano, with its sourness and acidity is a particularly great match for many foods.

**Nose** Dried cherries and an enticing earthiness dominate this classic Chianti nose.

**Mouth** Though its acidity might be a bit off-putting solo, the slight tanginess is nice.

**Design** That Tuscan warrior may be a bit over the top, but at least you won't forget what you're drinking. But "gabbiano" is the Italian word for "seagull," which makes the knight and lack of bird all the more intriguing.

# Gato Negro Malbec

Viña San Pedro

**$6**

**BARGAIN**

**Style** Heavy New World red
**Country** Chile **Vintage tasted** 2008
**Grapes** Malbec
**Drink with** beef empanadas, barbecue ribs
**Website** www.gatonegro.cl

We have a sneaking suspicion this brand name was chosen because it consists of two of the only non-food-related words anyone who's taken grade-school Spanish will remember. That decision seems to have worked well: Gato Negro is currently one of the larger Chilean brands. Maybe we're being unfair, though—this wine is pleasant and approachable enough to earn market share all by itself.

**Nose** Our blind tasters picked up on cherry, earth, and what one described as "road gravel."

**Mouth** It's medium-bodied with lingering red fruit, pepper, and chocolate. Delicious.

**Design** Well, it's a gato negro. At least they kept it simple; for a critter wine, it's not half bad. But we can't sign off on the merger of the two words with the capital "N"—that went out of style in the late 1980s, and hasn't come back—nor do we approve of the raised baseline of the lowercase letters

# Geyser Peak Sauvignon Blanc

$14

*Three-time Wine Trials selection*

**Style** Light New World white
**Country** USA (CA)  **Vintage tasted** 2008
**Grapes** Sauvignon Blanc
**Drink with** fruit salad, vegetable tempura
**Website** www.geyserpeakwinery.com

This three-time *Wine Trials* selection proudly proclaims its dedication to terroir. It's refreshing to see such a commitment from a winery that churns out hundreds of thousands of cases of wine a year. Perhaps it's all for show, but merely promoting the idea of terroir in America is worthwhile—and if our blind tasters loved the wine this many years in a row, perhaps Geyser Peak is on to something.

**Nose** It's less powerful than last year's effort, with vegetal aromas and the distinct Sauvignon Blanc smell.

**Mouth** There's some fruit here, along with grassiness, floral flavors, and refreshing tartness.

**Design** We applaud Geyser Peak's decision to keep it simple and refrain from throwing in a château or curlicue vines. Still, we can't help feeling that there's something missing.

# Gobelsburger Grüner Veltliner

$13

Kamptal

**Style** Light Old World white
**Country** Austria  **Vintage tasted** 2009
**Grapes** Grüner Veltliner
**Drink with** seafood cocktail, summer pasta dishes
**Website** www.gobelsburg.com

Grüner Veltliner is the darling of the wine geeks, a grape praised for its high acidity and bright flavors. The Gobelsburger version, while certainly zippy, has a bit more oomph than we're used to seeing in these wines. But we like that about it. And we like any excuse to drink a good Grüner Veltliner, so we're happy to introduce Gobelsburger into the fold.

**Nose** Sweet scents of flowers dominate, as well as some stone fruit and wet rock.

**Mouth** Here's where the wine takes off and takes shape. It's got the requisite acid, but then a sort of nice sweet-savory balance. It's a meaty Austrian wine.

**Design** The pale yellow of the label plays nicely against the green bottle. All in all, it's quite elegant. Take this bottle to a BYO restaurant, and you'll be the coolest kid there.

# Graffigna Centenario Malbec

**Style** Heavy New World red
**Country** Argentina  **Vintage tasted** 2007
**Grapes** Malbec
**Drink with** Porterhouse steak, buffalo burgers
**Website** www.graffignawines.com

We're not the only ones to think this Malbec is special: it was awarded gold medals in both the "Councours Mondial de Bruxelles 2010" and the Vinus 2010 contest. While we're generally skeptical about the utility of these contests, this time we're pretty sure the judges got it right—it's complex, balanced, and generally a superb wine for the price.

**Nose** Pepper, dried black fruit, cola, and earth are just a few of the aromas our blind tasters found.

**Mouth** There are herbs here, along with intense tannins that can be a bit off-putting but will make it a perfect partner for red meat.

**Design** Now that's just classy. An elegant single-letter logo, a dark bottle, and simple, well-chosen fonts; we'll be taking this one to a dinner party in the near future.

# Green Bridge Zinfandel

**$9**

**Style** Heavy New World red
**Country** USA (CA)  **Vintage tasted** 2008
**Grapes** Zinfandel
**Drink with** Thanksgiving dinner, Fourth of July grilling

Zinfandel is America's best claim to a national grape variety—though it seems also to have genetic ties to Croatian grapes as well as Italy's Primitivo. Still, the name Zinfandel and its signature style are thoroughly Californian. Only in recent decades has the wine begun to gain the respect it deserves. Unabashedly huge and fruity (but not necessarily jammy), it's as boisterous and unapologetic as the settlers who first cultivated it.

**Nose** This wine is restrained for a Zin, with berries, vegetables, and a smell that reminded one taster of a plastic pool toy.

**Mouth** It's impressively balanced, with sufficient acid and tannins to counter the ripe flavors.

**Design** The contrast between the hunter green and gray is pleasing, the font is elegant, and we like the coarse paper texture..

# Greg Norman Cabernet Merlot

**$15**

Limestone Coast

**Style** Heavy New World red
**Country** Australia  **Vintage tasted** 2007
**Grapes** Cabernet Sauvignon, Merlot
**Drink with** pork chops, Brussels sprouts
**Website** www.gregnormanestateswine.com

Like the golfer/owner himself, Greg Norman is a large and well-respected producer from Australia, and it earns its reputation with this offering. It's definitely an Australian wine (big, fruity, and enthusiastically New World in style), but it's fairly complex and thoroughly delicious. It even reminded one blind taster of Thanksgiving dinners past.

**Nose** Loads of fruit here, with some sweet spice and a distinct aroma that one blind taster labeled as varnish.

**Mouth** Another blind taster found elegant fruit and pumpkin pie. There's more acidity than one might expect, as well as meat-friendly tannins.

**Design** They're certainly not trying to win anyone over with what's on the outside of these bottles. The signature shark is on the label to remind us of the inimitable golfer behind the operation—Great White Shark is Norman's nickname

# Guigal Côtes du Rhône

$10

**Style** Light Old World white
**Country** France  **Vintage tasted** 2009
**Grapes** Viognier, Marsanne, Roussanne
**Drink with** goat cheese and crackers, bratwurst
**Website** www.guigal.com

A Guigal wine is generally a safe bet. One of the best-known names in the Côtes du Rhône, Guigal's wines range in price from the affordable to the astronomical. An attention to quality permeates even the lower price points, resulting in impressive offerings like this one. In the previous two editions, Guigal's red has performed best, but this year the white takes the lead—a bit of a surprise from a region that is known predominantly for red wine. This bottle might serve as your clue that the white wines of the Rhône are well worth exploring.

**Nose** It's aromatic and spring-like, with floral and citrus aromas.

**Mouth** Fruity and flowery, it has enough acid and citrus flavors to remain light and refreshing.

**Design** It's an amusing mix of old-school French fontage with the new-school desire to evoke a sense of place through nostalgic geographical imagery and sepia coloration.

# Happy Camper Cabernet Sauvignon  $9

**Style** Heavy New World red
**Country** USA (CA)  **Vintage tasted** 2008
**Grapes** Cabernet Sauvignon
**Drink with** shawarma, black bean burgers
**Website** www.happycamperwines.com

You can just feel the branding effort exuded by the Happy Camper website, which reads like a laundry list of focus-grouped slogans with exclamation points after each: "Happy Camper is a taste of freedom! Strike out for adventure and head to the horizon. In three varietals, Happy Camper is your ticket to the good times ahead! Life is an adventure. Don't forget the wine!" It's not the kind of bottle we'd grab from a grocery store shelf. Which made us question our biases when the brown bag came off and we realized that underneath this stereotypical grocery store Cab label was some pretty decent wine.

**Nose** It's quite herbaceous, with a chemical note that disturbed some of our blind tasters.

**Mouth** More acidic than we'd expect, it has flavors of dried berries.

**Design** We're pretty sure this label is the result of a dare. How else do you explain the color scheme and the unfortunately insect-like RV?

# Hayman & Hill Cabernet Sauvignon

Napa Valley

**Style** Heavy New World red
**Country** USA (CA)  **Vintage tasted** 2007
**Grapes** Cabernet Sauvignon, Petite Sirah, Syrah
**Drink with** steak, lamb chops, by itself

It's rare to find a Cabernet Sauvignon from the Napa Valley AVA under $15, much less one that's as classically delicious as this. It has all the qualities that have earned Napa fans across the world: tons of fruit flavor, an expansive mouthfeel, and a hint of black pepper. Even our blind tasters who are skeptical of the California style couldn't help but love it. It would be a great pairing with a juicy steak, but we'd be just as happy to drink it by itself—it's so big it feels like a full meal.

**Nose** Our blind tasters found currant, pepper, and even what was described as wet grass, an adjective combination more often attributed to white wine.

**Mouth** It's big and expansive, with massive body and plenty more fruit.

**Design** Classic and elegant, with plenty of white space, simple fonts, and that ampersand, which creates costly associations. It looks almost as expensive as it tastes, and we'd happily bring it to a dinner party.

# Hogue Cellars Pinot Grigio

Columbia Valley

 $10

**Style** Light New World white
**Country** USA (WA)  **Vintage tasted** 2008
**Grapes** Pinot Grigio, Chardonnay, Gewürztraminer, Chenin Blanc
**Drink with** whole roasted fish, grilled shrimp
**Website** www.hoguecellars.com

When we think of Pinot Grigio, the word that comes most often to mind is "pretty." These wines are generally not powerful or overly complex; instead, they charm with easy fruit flavors and floral aromas. This pleasant wine, from one of Washington State's largest wineries, is no exception. We wouldn't recommend cellaring it or trying to pair it with powerful foods, but it will make for a wonderful apéritif.

**Nose** It's pretty and subtle, with a sharp lemon quality, as well as apples and flowers.

**Mouth** It could use a bit more acid (it seems almost sweet without it), but the green apple flavors are delicious.

**Design** We've been longstanding fans of the sideways Hogue logo, although the color scheme makes it feel cheaper than most Hogues. You win some, you lose some.

# House Wine Red

*Three-time Wine Trials selection*

**Style** Heavy New World red  **Country** USA (WA)
**Vintage tasted** 2007  **Grapes** Cabernet Sauvignon, Merlot, Syrah, Malbec, Cabernet Franc, Zinfandel, Petit Verdot
**Drink with** pork chops and a fresh green salad
**Website** www.magnificentwine.com

Were it not for brown bags (and the fact that this wine performed wonderfully for the past two years), we probably never would have tried this bottle: a lot of these new trying-too-hard labels tend to suggest sugary plonk. Not here. If anything, it's a bit understated—its light berry and vegetable flavors and robust tannins make for an ideal red table wine. Which is appropriate for a brand positioning itself as a "house wine."

**Nose** It's fairly subtle, with berries, stone, and vegetal aromas.

**Mouth** It's got good fruit and enough tannin to help it stand up to fairly robust dishes. One blind taster also picked up on a Dr. Pepper flavor.

**Design** Perhaps it's the Magic-Marker-style aesthetic that's scaring restaurants away from actually pouring this as their house wine. It certainly isn't the wine.

# Hugel Gentil

Hugel et Fils

**Style** Aromatic Old World white
**Country** France  **Vintage tasted** 2008
**Grapes** Gewürztraminer, Pinot Gris, Muscat, Riesling, Sylvaner
**Drink with** green curry, Szechuan dishes
**Website** www.hugel.com

Alsace occupies an interesting place in the wine world: fought over for centuries between France and Germany, its wines reflect both countries but are markedly distinct. The region is particularly respected for its Gewürztraminer, an extremely aromatic grape that's almost as fun to drink as it is to say. Hugel et Fils is one of the largest (and best) of the Alsatian Gewürztraminer producers, and this inexpensive offering is an excellent example of what the grape is all about.

**Nose** Our blind tasters still managed to identify some vegetal aromas. One imaginative taster even smelled lemon Kool-Aid.

**Mouth** It has classic aromas of fresh citrus and stone, along with that Alsatian zingy acidity.

**Design** It's classic and looks extremely expensive—not surprising, given that the label is very similar to other Hugel offerings that are indeed expensive. Bring this one to your wine snob friend.

# Il Rosso di Enzo

Cantine Pirovano

**Style** Heavy Old World red
**Country** Italy  **Vintage tasted** 2009
**Grapes** Sangiovese, Negroamaro, Aglianico, Primitivo
**Drink with** grilled meat, meat-based pastas
**Website** www.vinicantinepirovano.com

Pirovano, which produces regional wines from every corner of Italy, is a frequent visitor to the pages of *The Wine Trials*. This is one of its better offerings, and it has a taste that's distinctly Old World Italian. We normally wouldn't trust an Italian wine that refuses to name its region of origin, but that's the beauty of blind tasting: despite our prejudices, it's impossible to argue with what's in the bottle. And what's in this bottle is very tasty indeed.

**Nose** It's got plenty of black fruit, earth, and a mulchy aroma—a combination that prompted one blind taster to say that it was subtle and smelled expensive.

**Mouth** It's smooth in the mouth, with cherries and continued earthiness. All in all, a perfect wine for outdoor grilling.

**Design** You'd think Old World wine producers would eventually run out of new heraldic crests to put on bottles. Apparently not.

# J. Lohr Estates Los Osos Merlot

Paso Robles

**Style** Heavy New World red
**Country** USA (CA)  **Vintage tasted** 2007
**Grapes** Merlot, Malbec, Petit Verdot, Cabernet Sauvignon
**Drink with** duck breast with plum sauce, grilled chicken
**Website** www.jlohr.com

We could go on for quite a while listing all the things we love about J. Lohr. The producer continues to make individual vineyard wines (rather than blending grapes from different sites) despite being a fairly large producer. The folks there are also proud sustainable growers who operate the wine world's largest solar panel array; it's certainly not every winery that can say it produces 75% of its own electricity. Best of all, J. Lohr produces some truly wonderful wines, with this juicy Merlot as one of the best.

**Nose** The blackberry here is so rich it seems cooked or jammy, but our blind tasters didn't mind a bit.

**Mouth** It's sleek and juicy in the mouth, with mild tannins and acidity. There's also a hint of herbs in there.

**Design** J. Lohr's bottles tend to be weighty and sleek, making them seem more expensive. The label's nothing special, but it doesn't interfere, either.

# J. Lohr Estates South Ridge Syrah
Paso Robles

**Style** Heavy New World red
**Country** USA (CA)  **Vintage tasted** 2007
**Grapes** Syrah, Petite Sirah, Grenache
**Drink with** game meat, hamburgers
**Website** www.jlohr.com

This wine is a wonderful reminder of the potential of the New World style. Dense berries and a ripe mouth can be wonderful, after all, so long as the wine remains balanced. While this wine might be on the upper end of our price spectrum, it tastes even more expensive, making it an impressive value.

**Nose** Our blind tasters identified blackberries, black currant, and a smoky, campfire aroma.

**Mouth** There's chocolate here, as well as vegetal flavors and a plush smoothness that fooled some of our blind tasters into identifying this as a Merlot.

**Design** Just as this wine exemplifies the good New World stuff, J. Lohr embodies the California aesthetic—a rendering of the vineyard and a strictly business label wrap with all the crucial info.

# J.P. Chenet Blanc de Blancs Brut

**$12**

WINNER

**Style** Sparkling
**Country** France  **Vintage tasted** Non-Vintage
**Grapes** Airén, Ugni Blanc
**Drink with** dim sum, buttered lobster
**Website** www.jpchenet.com

Typically Blanc de Blancs means that a sparkling wine is composed entirely of Chardonnay (as opposed to the blend of Chardonnay, Pinot Noir, and Pinot Meunier that makes up most Champagne), but J.P. Chenet intends the term literally: this is a white sparkling wine made up of a "blend of white grapes." What the makers are putting in is clearly working, as our blind tasters loved this effort. It's crisp, with loads of the intense acidity that can turn an ordinary sparkler into a refreshing summer delight.

**Nose** It's light, with faint floral aromas and a smell one blind taster compared to apple pie.

**Mouth** Some of our tasters thought they detected initial sweetness, but it was quickly washed away by the acidity.

**Design** While we applaud the makers for trying something new, the strange melted-glass-meets-funhouse-mirror made us feel a bit queasy.

# Jacob's Creek Reserve Pinot Noir
## South Australia

**Style** Light New World red
**Country** Australia  **Vintage tasted** 2007
**Grapes** Pinot Noir
**Drink with** hamburgers, cassoulet
**Website** www.jacobscreek.com

*The Wine Trials* tends to give the Aussies a hard time, and often for good reason—too frequently, the overripeness and cheap oak flavors of many inexpensive Australian wines ruins their potential. Still, there's a reason they were once the darlings of the wine world: they have some incredible terroir and old vines. So when we taste a delicious wine like this, made from the famously difficult Pinot Noir grape and from one of the country's larger producers, we're excited. Keep 'em coming, guys.

**Nose** No one will ever mistake this for a Burgundy (the classic French expression of this grape): it's super fruity, with lots of red berries. It's not overwhelming, though.

**Mouth** More berries here; it's big for a Pinot, but not unpleasantly so.

**Design** There's something about the elegance of the bottle shape of Pinot Noir that warms our hearts. And the label design doesn't interfere with that, which is good enough.

# Kaiken Reserve Malbec

Mendoza

**Style** Heavy New World red
**Country** Argentina  **Vintage tasted** 2007
**Grapes** Malbec, Cabernet Sauvignon
**Drink with** steak au poivre, shish kebab
**Website** www.kaikenwines.com

Kaikenes are wild geese in Patagonia that routinely fly back and forth between Argentina and Chile. This winery was begun by a Chilean producer who moved to start a new venture in Argentina, so he named the wine after the geese. Romantic, no?

**Nose** It's not a showoff, but its simple aromas of berries and earth pleased our tasters.

**Mouth** A perfect table wine, it has straightforward fruit one blind taster called lovely. For a Malbec, it has a surprisingly supple feel.

**Design** It's very clean and sharp at first glance, but more confusing once you look closely. The font is nice and looks almost Japanese—this could pass for a sake label.

# Kourtaki Mavrodaphne of Patras

*Three-time Wine Trials selection*

**Style** Sweet Old World red
**Country** Greece  **Vintage tasted** Non-Vintage
**Grapes** Mavrodaphne
**Drink with** crème brûlée, Raisinets, chocolate ganache
**Website** www.kourtakis.com

We imagine this is what sweet wine tasted like a thousand years ago. Rich, raisiny, and rustic, this Greek wine (and repeat *Wine Trials* selection) is the kind of thing Odysseus would have drunk to celebrate his return. Even better, a slight deliberate oxidation means that you can keep the bottle open for a few days and the wine won't change—something you'd have to be crazy to attempt with most non-fortified wines.

**Nose** Our blind tasters found it rich and decadent, with aromas of caramel, apricot, toffee, and raisin. The slight aroma of alcohol is a bit distracting, but we're not complaining.

**Mouth** It's dark and viscous, with flavors of raisin, chocolate, toffee, and nuts.

**Design** It's all cheesy Grecophilia, from the fonts to the gold medallion. At least the balance of white, red, black, and gold is soothing.

# La Vieille Ferme Blanc

**Côtes du Ventoux AOC**

$8

**Style** Light Old World white
**Country** France  **Vintage tasted** 2009
**Grapes** Grenache Blanc, Bourboulenc, Ugni Blanc, Roussanne
**Drink with** grilled sea bass, insalata caprese
**Website** www.lavieilleferme.com

For two years, the red wine from this producer has wowed our tasters; now it's the white's turn. Ugni Blanc, a part of this blend, is the most widely planted grape in France (often known as Trebbiano in Italy). It makes wines like this one: fresh, fruity, and meant for immediate consumption. So don't give this bottle to your mother if she's likely to save it for a special occasion a few years down the road—it won't end well.

**Nose** It's aromatic, with peach, orange, and floral notes. There's also some nice minerality.

**Mouth** It's very light here, almost to the point of being thin. But the orange and lime flavors and refreshing acidity save it.

**Design** Don't be fooled by the fake French handwriting or the homeliness of the chicken couple flirting on the bottle; Perrin, the Rhône giant, is behind this big brand.

# Lagaria Merlot
Sicilia IGT

$10

**Style** Heavy Old World red
**Country** Italy  **Vintage tasted** 2008
**Grapes** Merlot
**Drink with** duck confit, beef tacos

You might never have thought of Southern Italy as great Merlot country, but maybe this wine will change your mind. In sharp contrast to many New World Merlots, which can be overly fruity and uninteresting, this one has a strong hit of earthiness and barnyard (though there's plenty of fruit as well). Again and again our blind tasters kept coming up with words like elegant to describe it.

**Nose** There's black fruit, some cherry, and an aroma one blind taster compared to wet earth.

**Mouth** Smooth and "elegant," it has fruit, earth, and herbs. One blind taster also identified what she called "Christmas-spice flavors."

**Design** The still life is classy, if a bit 18th century.

# Lâl Rosé
Kavaklidere

**WINNER $10**

**Style** Rosé
**Country** Turkey  **Vintage tasted** 2008
**Grapes** Çalkarisi
**Drink with** cold shrimp, steamed lobster
**Website** www.kavaklidere.com

While few Americans have tasted Turkish wine, Turkey has a long tradition of winemaking. In fact, many historians believe that winemaking began in this region. Kavaklidere is the country's largest producer but a respected one, with wines that range from age-worthy reds to this steely, refreshing rosé, which reminds us of the wonderfully refreshing rosé from Provence in both its salmon color and its crisp flavor profile. This is a surprisingly rare treat in American wine stores, where a lot of rosé is looking more and more like Pinot Noir these days.

**Nose** Our blind tasters loved the muted, mineral nose with faint fruit and an impression of chalk.

**Mouth** It's steely, with some light fruit and wonderful acidity.

**Design** This label looks as if it were generated with Microsoft Word, and we could certainly do without the hot pink stripe at the top. This is one of the *Wine Trials 2011* bottles most in need of Label 911.

# Lan Rioja Crianza

*Three-time Wine Trials selection*

**Style** Light Old World red
**Country** Spain  **Vintage tasted** 2006
**Grapes** Tempranillo
**Drink with** seared duck breast, pork tenderloin
**Website** www.bodegaslan.com

Last edition's *Wine Trials* winner put in another stellar performance this year, with earthy and fruity notes that combine to create what one blind taster could only call "a very special wine." It's this sort of bottle—unique, rich, expressive, and extremely affordable—that has us head over heels for Rioja, the kind old uncle of wine regions. Here's to hoping the folks at Lan keep up the good work.

**Nose** Our blind tasters smelled sour cherries, herbs, undergrowth, mulch, mushrooms—above all, they agreed that it smelled expensive.

**Mouth** It's herbal and rustic, with enough tannins to help it pair well with food. But there's also juicy red fruit; this wine just has it all.

**Design** Distressed yellow paper creates a nice backdrop for the royal red. It looks dated, but then, so is the region, and we're not complaining.

# Les Hauts de Janeil Syrah Grenache  $13
François Lurton

**Style** Heavy Old World red
**Country** France  **Vintage tasted** 2008
**Grapes** Syrah, Grenache, Cinsault, Carignan
**Drink with** lamb burgers, beef enchilada
**Website** www.francoislurton.com

Our blind tasters fell in love with quite a few of these types of Rhône blends this year, and it's a style that is now being made more elegantly than previously in the inexpensive wine market. Syrah, with its herbal, meaty flavors, makes the perfect yin to Grenache's fruity, approachable yang. This wine is a stellar example, with an impressive balance of earthiness and fruit. It's a great reminder of why we blend wines to begin with.

**Nose** Pepper and earth from the Syrah side; blackberry jam from the Grenache. Like we said, it's a tempting mélange.

**Mouth** There are some berries here, along with rough tannins from the Syrah. It's more of a food wine than a porch sipper.

**Design** This tree-meets-Jackson Pollock-meets-wine-spill is one of the coolest labels we've ever seen. They even get away with the freestyle cursive, which in lesser hands just looks silly.

# Louis Latour Le Pinot Noir

*Three-time Wine Trials selection*

**Style** Light Old World red
**Country** France  **Vintage tasted** 2007
**Grapes** Pinot Noir
**Drink with** pork chops, lentil soup
**Website** www.louislatour.com

If Bordeaux and Napa are the intro courses of wine—relatively easy to understand and indispensable for wine drinkers—then Burgundy is the master class. Its famously confusing appellation system and uneven vintages can baffle even the most devoted student. Thankfully, the mass producer Louis Latour has provided a cheat sheet for the confused and intimidated: its approachable style (athough its future is threatened if the upward trend in price continues) and easy-to-understand labeling should help even the least knowledgeable.

**Nose** It abandons earthy elements in favor of light cherry and raspberry.

**Mouth** It's simple and young (as you'd expect from an entry-level Burgundy), but delicious. There's also a nice level of acidity.

**Design** We're not huge fans of the script logo, but at least there are no goofy animals here. Still, Louis Latour's classic labels, which try less hard, are much better.

# Lungarotti Fiamme

Umbria Rosso IGT

$14

**Style** Light Old World red
**Country** Italy  **Vintage tasted** 2008
**Grapes** Sangiovese, Merlot
**Drink with** barbecue ribs, flank steak, spaghetti alla bolognese
**Website** www.lungarotti.it

Umbria borders Tuscany, and with its greener fields and craggier mountains it's one of the few regions of Italy that can give its neighbor competition in the charming landscapes department. Apparently Lungarotti hopes to compete in the Old-World-meets-New wine department as well: this wine is clearly modeled on the so-called Super Tuscans—powerful and usually expensive wines made by blending traditional grapes with international ones. And while this bottle may not have the punch of premium Super Tuscans, it's a wonderfully elegant table wine.

**Nose** Bright and clear, it has berry and vegetal aromas.

**Mouth** Simple, rustic, and as one blind taster put it, a perfect example of an Italian table wine.

**Design** Fiamme is the Italian word for flames, so we shouldn't be too harsh on the red-and-black color scheme. But did the cartoon fire have to be drawn by a five-year old?

# Lurton Pinot Gris

Bodega Lurton, Valle de Eco

**Style** Light New World white
**Country** Argentina  **Vintage tasted** 2009
**Grapes** Pinot Gris
**Drink with** sushi, strawberries
**Website** www.francoislurton.com

The Lurtons are not exactly newcomers to wine: André and Lucien Lurton are some of the biggest players in Bordeaux, with holdings in the ultra-prestigious châteaux of D'Yquem and Cheval Blanc. André's son, François, decided to go his own way and purchase a number of wineries throughout the world; with this bottle he proves that he doesn't need to replicate the flash of his parents' offerings. This Pinot Gris is a perfect summer wine, the kind that evoked memories of past picnics in many of our blind tasters.

**Nose** A citrus nose of lemons and oranges is exactly what we crave in the heat.

**Mouth** It's almost prickly, enough to remind our blind tasters of a Vinho Verde—another great picnic wine.

**Design** The simplicity of the layout makes the ornate script seem attractive rather than precious. As always, it's a matter of detail.

# Madame Fleur Rosé

Vin de Pays d'Oc

**Style** Rosé
**Country** France  **Vintage tasted** 2008
**Grapes** Gamay, Cabernet Franc
**Drink with** shellfish, cheese plate

Our answer to the proverbial what-would-you-want-with-you-on-a-desert-island question just might be a good French rosé. With more oomph than your average white, but not the heaviness of your average red, they're just about right for prolonged periods of imbibing in the sun. And the color is a delight on its own: the pale salmon pink of a good rosé looks almost as refreshing as it tastes.

**Nose** A hint of mashed strawberry is a refreshing whiff, and there's an aroma of flowers that is lovely and not cloying.

**Mouth** Big savory aromas don't tread lightly, but you won't mind that. A decent burst of acid counterbalances nicely the bright, fresh, young fruit aromas. Now where's our beach house already?

**Design** Flowers, water, fields, and a lazy sky do their impressionist best to whisk you away. But the square "365" logo snaps you right back into the realm of everyday value.

# Malenchini Chianti

Chianti DOCG

**Style** Light Old World red
**Country** Italy  **Vintage tasted** 2007
**Grapes** Sangiovese
**Drink with** cheese and prosciutto, chicken with stewed tomatoes

One of a few Chiantis to make this year's *Wine Trials*, this wine fits perfectly into the Chianti mold. It has a distinctive aroma of animals and manure that is euphemistically labeled "barnyard," but enough red fruit to please most New World drinkers. Drinking it, we can't help but think of little farmhouses in Tuscany and plates piled high with freshly made pasta.

**Nose** Red fruit, dried herbs, barnyard, a little spice.

**Mouth** Our blind tasters appreciated the continuing fruit, as well as the hint of leather and the lean acidity that will help it pair with tomato dishes.

**Design** The super-dark bottle is a bit imposing, but it makes a nice contrast against the gold outline of the label. For once, gold that isn't gaudy! We can't get behind the larger "N" in the middle of "Malenchini," however; it ruins the spirit of the nostalgic font.

# Man Vintners Cabernet Sauvignon

## Coastal Region

**Style** Heavy New World red
**Country** South Africa  **Vintage tasted** 2008
**Grapes** Cabernet Sauvignon
**Drink with** steak, barbecued brisket, grilled pork sausage
**Website** www.manvintners.com

These guys have some great slogans. Their official word on this Cab is that "this is the opposite of a critter wine, this is a wine to drink with critters." Maybe it's just marketing savvy and they've only latched on to the backlash against over-oaked, over-cute critter wines, but either way we like their sense of humor. And the wine's not bad either. It's as bold and brash as their attitude, with plenty of New World punch but without the worst excesses of the critter epidemic.

**Nose** The combination of berries and a smoky, burnt aroma led one taster to compare this wine to "scorched red fruit." Another taster was reminded of barbecue.

**Mouth** Smoke, red fruit, and chocolate form a big New World flavor profile.

**Design** We love the simplicity here. Also, that little guy looks distinctly like the South Africa World Cup mascot—coincidence?

# Man Vintners Chenin Blanc
Coastal Region

**Style** Aromatic New World white
**Country** South Africa  **Vintage tasted** 2009
**Grapes** Chenin Blanc
**Drink with** Caesar salad, chicken sandwich
**Website** www.manvintners.com

We love these vintners. Clearly after our own hearts, they tout their hardy "extreme terroir," insisting that the hostile environment leads to flavorful, powerful grapes. We're inclined to agree—this Chenin Blanc (one of a few in this year's edition) is quite dry and acidic but still full bodied. Let's hope other winemakers follow their straight-shooting lead.

**Nose** It has a funky nose, which surprised our blind tasters with some oak.

**Mouth** It's clean and slightly metallic, with a round mouthfeel cut by bracing acidity.

**Design** As they said, there's no critter here—though that squiggly guy looks suspiciously adorable…

# Mania Rueda

**Bodegas Felix Lorenzo Cachazo**

$14

**Style** Light Old World white
**Country** Spain  **Vintage tasted** 2009
**Grapes** Viura, Verdejo
**Drink with** sole, soft French cheeses
**Website** www.mundiserv.com/cachazo

This blend of two Spanish light white grapes (Viura and Verdejo) is crisp, fruity, and extremely likeable. It may not bowl you over with complex aromas or intense flavors, but it's fresh and will go equally well with a hot day or a simple fish course. Anyone who would turn their noses up at a wine like this clearly hasn't spent time with a chilled bottle on a summer afternoon.

**Nose** It's floral and fruity, with refreshing citrus.

**Mouth** There's more citrus here, with just enough acidity to counter the fruit. One blind taster even detected a slight, refreshing prickle.

**Design** From the butterfly-within-a-butterfly to the through-the-bottle label view, this design is innovative and attractive. We're definitely fans.

# Mark West Pinot Noir

*Three-time Wine Trials selection*

**Style** Light New World red
**Country** USA (CA)  **Vintage tasted** 2008
**Grapes** Pinot Noir
**Drink with** fried chicken, roast pork
**Website** www.markwestwines.com

The revolution marches on: with their wine appearing for the third time in *The Wine Trials*, the comrades at Mark West continue to fight their Pinot for the People campaign (and to maintain a faux-Marxist website that's worth checking out). Their manifesto demands "rich, fruit-inspired, easy-drinking wine," and this lush Pinot is nothing if not easy-drinking. It remains to be seen whether these wines will topple class divisions or foment international uprisings, but we can't wait see what Mark West's Five-Year-Plan has in store.

**Nose** True to their words, the folks at Mark West have turned out a lush wine filled with red fruit.

**Mouth** The fruit is so ripe it almost seems cooked. But it's hard to fault them for delivering on a promise.

**Design** This bottle is dangerously bourgeois; the playfulness of the website doesn't translate to the design, which is all business and tasteful maroon.

# Marqués de Cáceres Rioja

*Two-time Wine Trials selection*

**$15**

**Style** Light Old World red
**Country** Spain  **Vintage tasted** 2006
**Grapes** Tempranillo, Garnacha, Graciano
**Drink with** brisket, stuffed mushrooms
**Website** www.marquesdecaceres.com

Everybody knows Marqués de Cáceres, either in its white, red, or pink form; it might well be the mostly widely distributed Spanish brand in the U.S. In previous editions this producer's white wine was a favorite, but this year the red stole the show. It's restrained, earthy, and food-friendly—exactly what a cheap Spanish red should be.

**Nose** Remember when you were a kid and you wanted a pony? Well, this wine smells like a stable, which is the next best thing. We suppose. There's also red fruit that lends an approachability to all the earthiness.

**Mouth** Our blind tasters loved its sleekness, as well as the delicate balance of tannin and acid.

**Design** Well, at least they're not trying to be trendy. The design might be a bit outdated, but it certainly works better with the red wine than with their white.

# Matua Pinot Noir
Marlborough

**Style** Light New World red
**Country** New Zealand  **Vintage tasted** 2008
**Grapes** Pinot Noir
**Drink with** duck breast, vegetable stew
**Website** www.matua.co.nz

New Zealand Pinot Noirs have wine lovers very excited. So far Marlborough Pinots seem to be well balanced, interesting, and to have a real sense of place—and they get better every year. Matua's offering definitely fits that mold: there's a lot of red fruit, but also lots of acidity, and the wine maintains a balance that's rare in New World Pinots in this price range. It may not be Burgundy (yet), but we're excited to see what this region can do.

**Nose** There are big aromas of red berries, along with a touch of earthiness and an aroma that one blind taster identified as cream soda.

**Mouth** There are more berries here, balanced by appealing acidity. It should be delicious by itself or with food.

**Design** Yikes, what a color scheme. Perhaps this is Matua's grand plan to get its wines placed in hotel mini-bars across the US by matching the awful colors low-end hotel chains so love.

# Mionetto Il Prosecco
Treviso DOC

**$10**

**Style** Sparkling
**Country** Italy  **Vintage tasted** Non-Vintage
**Grapes** Prosecco
**Drink with** a great party, bruschetta
**Website** www.mionettousa.com

Show us someone who dislikes Prosecco, and we'll show you either a liar or a curmudgeon (or both). These sparklers may not have the complexity of fine Champagne or the refreshing bite of Spanish Cava, but they are fruity, aromatic, and undeniably pleasurable to drink. And a glass of chilled Prosecco makes the perfect reward for a day spent overseeing the planting on the lawn in front of your faux-Tuscan suburban villa

**Nose** Bright citrus, tropical fruit, and an appealing grapiness combine pleasantly.

**Mouth** It's a perfectly pleasant blend of tropical fruit and decent acidity (though some of our blind tasters wished there had been more acid).

**Design** The bottle shape and metal cap could easily lead you to believe this is an exotic beer. We like the single, elegant swoosh (look carefully and you'll notice it's the Italian definite article "il").

# Mohua Sauvignon Blanc

Marlborough

$13

**Style** Light New World white
**Country** New Zealand  **Vintage tasted** 2009
**Grapes** Sauvignon Blanc
**Drink with** whole grilled fish, fried oysters

New Zealand Sauvignon Blanc has a very distinctive profile, and this one has every characteristic there is: tropical fruit, check; vegetable flavors, check; refreshingly sharp acidity, check. If you like that general profile, you'll love this wine. On the other hand, Kiwi haters should definitely beware—this is not for any half-hearted Sauv Blanc drinkers. If you're not sure which camp you fall in, have a glass of this: you'll quickly find out.

**Nose** Our blind tasters found plenty of those aforementioned tropical fruits and "cat pee."

**Mouth** There's still fruit here, but it's balanced by a distinctly grassy, vegetal note that can be off-putting for some drinkers.

**Design** We love this design. It's classy, harmonious, and the bird image works well—it's a better critter than a furry mammal. And the green color is appropriate for the wine.

# MontAsolo Merlot

Veneto IGT

**Style** Light Old World red
**Country** Italy  **Vintage tasted** 2008
**Grapes** Merlot
**Drink with** chicken Provençal, spanakopita

Anyone who thinks of a Merlot as a natural fruit bomb should try this wine from northern Italy: there's not a fruit flavor in sight. Instead, the wine is earthy, vegetal, and even piney. It might take some getting used to (and we'd miss our fruit if this was all we drank), but it's certainly an interesting change from New World Merlot.

**Nose** There are vegetable notes (especially green pepper), and an aroma one blind taster compared to a pine tree.

**Mouth** It's distinctly rustic, with herbs, nuts, and more vegetal flavors.

**Design** The cursive script needs to go back to where it came from—the awning of a strip-mall nail salon in suburbia. And we've definitely seen that shade of red on the cover of a romance novel.

# Monte Antico

Toscana IGT

**$12 WINNER**

**Style** Light Old World red
**Country** Italy  **Vintage tasted** 2006
**Grapes** Sangiovese, Merlot, Cabernet Sauvignon
**Drink with** roast duck, meat stew
**Website** www.monteanticowine.com

Once upon a time, most serious producers in Tuscany adhered rigidly to the region's strict guidelines, which stipulated that high-level reds be made of regional grapes (mainly Sangiovese). Then it was discovered that wines that included international varieties such as Merlot and Cabernet Sauvignon could be sold for enormous sums, even if they were legally designated as IGT or table wines—and so was born the so-called "Super Tuscan." While the Monte Antico red is below the price point associated with the name, and is thankfully less concentrated as well, it does take the Super Tuscans as its model.

**Nose** Our blind tasters identified dirt, black cherry, smoke, and leather.

**Mouth** There are more cherries here, along with earth, herbs, and a nice hit of tannin.

**Design** It's a bit text-heavy and has the clichéd vineyard sketch, but otherwise we like the simple, rustic feel.

# Montecillo Rioja Crianza

*Two-time Wine Trials selection*

**Style** Light Old World red
**Country** Spain  **Vintage tasted** 2006
**Grapes** Tempranillo
**Drink with** jamón serrano, grilled sausage
**Website** www.osborne.es

Rioja has exacting legal standards governing winemaking; whether a wine qualifies as a crianza, reserva, gran reserva, or merely a plain Rioja is dictated by requirements of aging, grape type, and production volume. Crianza is the second rung up on Rioja's hierarchy, denoting a wine that has been aged for at least two years, with at least six months in oak barrels. While these wines normally have earthy aromas, this one is much more fruit-forward in style.

**Nose** We hope you like cherry. Our blind tasters identified candied cherries, sour cherries, and chocolate-covered cherries. There's also a slight, pleasing animal aroma.

**Mouth** Though its flavors of malted chocolate and cherries may sound sweet, this wine isn't at all.

**Design** A red-and-black color scheme, winery crest, flowing script next to block lettering, vineyard illustration, and gold gilding—clearly this winery believes we're still in the Spanish Golden Age.

# Monthaven Merlot
## Underdog Wine Merchants

**Style** Heavy New World red
**Country** USA (CA)  **Vintage tasted** 2007
**Grapes** Merlot, Petite Sirah, Petit Verdot
**Drink with** hamburgers, mushrooms stuffed with cheese
**Website** www.underdogwinemerchants.com

The boxes are doing extremely well this year, reflecting the fact that you can increasingly find very decent table wines wrapped in cardboard. This one is impressively complex for a Merlot at this price point, and we certainly wouldn't feel at all ashamed to pour it for company—though we might recommend hiding it in a giant three-liter brown paper bag.

**Nose** Vegetables, dried cherries, spice, and even dried flowers make an appearance. Very impressive.

**Mouth** More cherry, herbs, and vegetables. It's also a bit tannic, with acidity that our blind tasters figured would be great with food.

**Design** We love the Octavin shape (octagonal rather than rectangular) as it seems infinitely sleeker than the old boxy design. Other than that, there's not much to recommend this design, aside from the pleasant Monthaven font— perhaps you could use it as a mirror?

# Nobilo Sauvignon Blanc

Marlborough • *Three-time Wine Trials selection*

**Style** Light New World white
**Country** New Zealand  **Vintage tasted** 2009
**Grapes** Sauvignon Blanc
**Drink with** fried clams, roast chicken
**Website** www.nobilowines.com

Nobilo was founded in the 1940s by a Croatian immigrant whose family had been making wine in Europe for hundreds of years. According to the story, he moved to New Zealand in hopes of continuing to make wines in the Old World style—the likes of which were nowhere to be found in Kiwi country. There's still work to be done: just like last year's vintage, whose flavors were most definitely not European, this year's wine has many of the green, less fruity flavors we associate with New World Sauvignon Blanc.

**Nose** Our blind tasters found vegetal aromas (especially cabbage) and lime—not a bad combination at all.

**Mouth** Sharp and acidic, it has lots of vegetal flavors and a bit of fruit as well.

**Design** It's simple and unusually refined for the New World, with a pleasing color combination and regal fonts.

# Norton Cabernet Sauvignon

Mendoza • *Two-time Wine Trials selection*

**Style** Heavy New World red
**Country** Argentina **Vintage tasted** 2009
**Grapes** Cabernet Sauvignon
**Drink with** hearty stews, meatloaf
**Website** www.norton.com.ar

The Cabernet was just one of four Norton wines to make last year's cut for *The Wine Trials* and contribute to the producer's victory as Winery of the Year. Located in Luján de Cuyo in Mendoza, the British-Swiss-run winery is producing some of the most widely available Argentine wines in the US market. Combine that with their booming enotourism business, and you can't question their winemaking skills—or their marketing savvy.

**Nose** It's definitely woodsy. One blind taster even called this wine foxy.

**Mouth** It's elegant and balanced, with chocolate and pepper. Underneath, there's a layer of supporting fruit that's subtle and delicious.

**Design** Simple as can be. The design is clean and understated. Bodegas Norton doesn't need an army of animals to catch consumers' eyes from the shelves.

# Norton Malbec

**$11**

Mendoza • *Two-time Wine Trials selection*

**Style** Heavy New World red
**Country** Argentina  **Vintage tasted** 2009
**Grapes** Malbec
**Drink with** smoked turkey, strip steak
**Website** www.norton.com.ar

These days, the connection in many consumers' minds between Argentina and Malbec is indelible. Known as the quality grape from a bargain region, Malbec has made a New World name for itself. It's quite common in France, in the Cahors region, where inky black wines are made primarily from Malbec. Its Argentine incarnations are usually fairly big, tannic, and practically crying out to be drunk with a big juicy steak.

**Nose** There are tons of berries here, and one blind taster identified some wood as well.

**Mouth** It's tighter than the nose, and quite green, or vegetal. A healthy dose of tannin and excellent balance suggest it will be a great food wine.

**Design** It's boring, but in a good way. There's nothing for us to pick on, and we most certainly don't mind being nice.

# Oggi Pinot Grigio

Veneto IGT

**Style** Aromatic Old World white
**Country** Italy **Vintage tasted** 2008
**Grapes** Pinot Grigio
**Drink with** fruit salad, pan-seared fish

This one was a crowd pleaser, and it kept our blind tasters busy naming the exotic aromas and flavors hidden within. There's an impression of sugar here, so sweets-haters beware; otherwise, the wine is quite inoffensive. We recommend that you follow the makers' suggestion ("oggi" is the Italian word for "today"), and have a bottle as soon as possible.

**Nose** It's extremely aromatic, with aromas that our blind tasters identified as peach, roses, spice, orange, and flowers.

**Mouth** There are more peach and floral flavors here, although our blind tasters would have liked a bit more acid.

**Design** What a cheery label. The orange circles make us think of fireflies on a summer night. Which is when this should be drunk.

# Opala Vinho Verde

**Style** Light Old World white
**Country** Portugal  **Vintage tasted** 2009
**Grapes** Trajadura, Avessa
**Drink with** grilled crawfish, a picnic

As you might have noticed, we love our Vinho Verde. That's not just bias: the combination of their easy-to-like style, rock bottom prices, impressive consistency, and refreshing essence make it a hit with our blind tasters. This wine, a particularly good reminder of why we like Vinho Verde so much, has been getting raves in the wine blogosphere for quite a while. But don't just take our word for it; at $9, it's easy enough to sit out on the porch and try a chilled bottle yourself.

**Nose** It's fairly faint, but concentrate and you'll pick up apples, peach, and a great floral aroma.

**Mouth** Crisp, refreshing acidity, clean flavors, and a slight effervescent prickle—it's a Vinho Verde, all right.

**Design** The lightweight font and green vines look as young and fresh as the bottle's contents. Here's to maintaining a green lifestyle.

# Oro de Castilla

Rueda, Hermanos del Villar

**Style** Light Old World white
**Country** Spain  **Vintage tasted** 2009
**Grapes** Verdejo
**Drink with** grilled calamari, pasta salad
**Website** www.orodecastilla.com

This wine has excellent pedigree: the Rueda region has been producing Verdejo since receiving a grant by King Alfonso VI in the 11th century. For centuries it was a famous source of this fresh white wine, until a blight of disease (the infamous phylloxera louse) destroyed most of the vines; the region has been recovering ever since. Hermanos del Villar gives us a hint of what those wines might have tasted like—and who would say no to a taste of history for $14?

**Nose** Impressively complex and aromatic, it has tropical fruits (including papaya), and vegetal, stone fruit, and floral aromas.

**Mouth** Though some of our blind tasters found it a bit too low in acidity (and thus a bit flabby), they all liked the green apple and pineapple.

**Design** The abstract design in the background adds some spice without drawing too much attention. We get the feeling it stands for something, but—other than the obvious tree symbol—we're not sure what.

# Oyster Bay Sauvignon Blanc

**$13**

Marlborough • *Three-time Wine Trials selection*

**Style** Light New World white
**Country** New Zealand  **Vintage tasted** 2009
**Grapes** Sauvignon Blanc
**Drink with** fish and chips, grilled shrimp
**Website** www.oysterbaywines.com

One of the best-known and most popular Kiwi wines, Oyster Bay is very distinctively a New Zealand Sauvignon Blanc. While it doesn't have much of the "cat pee" flavor that often distinguishes these wines, it has all the tropical fruit, biting acidity, and vegetal flavors you could ask for. That's not surprising, as we find these wines to be some of the most consistent in the wine world at this price point; if you like the style you'll rarely be disappointed.

**Nose** Our blind tasters found floral aromas, tropical fruit, apple, and cabbage—in a good way.

**Mouth** It's consistent here, too: banana and other tropical fruits, vegetal flavors, and lots of acidity.

**Design** The label seems to be influenced by Hallmark sympathy cards. Also, is it just us or does that bay look like more of a cove?

# Parducci Sustainable Red

*Three-time Wine Trials selection*

**Style** Heavy New World red
**Country** USA (CA)  **Vintage tasted** 2006
**Grapes** Zinfandel, Syrah, Cabernet Sauvignon, Carignan
**Drink with** lamb chops, pecan pie
**Website** www.parducci.com

As the name implies, Parducci is committed to sustainable winemaking—though this seems to lead to major variations from vintage to vintage. This three-time winner was vegetal in our first edition, syrupy and fruity in our second, and this year it's meaty and savory but still fruity. We can't complain too much: this year's effort might be the best of the bunch, and it's nice to know you're doing your part to support sustainable practices.

**Nose** Our blind tasters said it jumps out at you with plum, meaty aromas, and sweet spice.

**Mouth** Sweet spice and fruit dominate the taste profile, too, and there's also a savory quality. Our blind tasters thought it tasted expensive.

**Design** The tree-like vine is lovingly rendered—the idea, of course, is to imagine that it's from one of the family-owned farms where the wine's grapes are grown.

# Pascual Toso Malbec

**$13**

Maipú • *Two-time Wine Trials selection*

**Style** Heavy New World red
**Country** Argentina  **Vintage tasted** 2009
**Grapes** Malbec
**Drink with** Texas chili, red-sauce pastas
**Website** www.bodegastoso.com.ar

Aside from this line of single-varietal wines, Pascual Toso produces some sparkling wines and a high-end line, Magdalena Toso, whose bottles are priced well above the cut-off for this guide. There's also a Malbec rosé, whose color is a radioactive hot pink, not the pale salmon color one looks for in a rosé. We'll stick with this repeat-winner Malbec—our blind tasters found it alternately fruity and earthy, and it's easy to imagine drinking it with a juicy steak.

**Nose** One blind taster focused on its ripe, jammy fruit, while another found earth and tea leaves.

**Mouth** The fruit lingers into an impressively long finish.

**Design** An elegant bottle, it looks like it's concealing some important contents. The smart design is something you would expect of a more expensive wine, but we all know that money doesn't buy class.

# Pölka Dot Riesling
Pfalz

$12

**Style** Aromatic Old World white
**Country** Germany  **Vintage tasted** 2008
**Grapes** Riesling
**Drink with** roast pork, spicy Indian curries
**Website** www.polkadotwines.com

This wine is from the Pfalz, one of the largest wine regions of Germany. It's an area rich in historical significance: grapes were first planted here by the Romans, and there were so many castles and minor princes in the area that the region's name is derived from the Latin word for "palace." And while we're pretty sure "Pölka Dot" isn't the name of old Germanic royalty, we're firm believers in the greatness of German wine—if adopting a silly Anglophone name is what it takes to win American devotees, we won't complain.

**Nose** A great German Riesling nose: lime, stone, and flowers compete for attention.

**Mouth** It's slightly sweet, with strong minerality, flowers, peaches, and good, cleansing acidity.

**Design** While we like the rich blue color in theory, we can't help thinking the bottle looks cheaper than it needs to: it's housing German Riesling, not wine spritzer, after all.

# Principipessa Gavia

Gavi DOCG

**$14**

**Style** Light Old World white
**Country** Italy **Vintage tasted** 2008
**Grapes** Cortese
**Drink with** white fish with lemon, fresh garden salad
**Website** www.vigneregali.com

The fairytale love story on the back of the bottle, which begins "Once upon a time…there lived a young princess named Gavia," is too saccharine to be believed. Do they really think this is what female drinkers want? We won't spoil the ending, but it's worth buying the bottle not to get the rest of the story, but for what's inside, which is considerably more exciting, with delicious fruit and bright acid.

**Nose** Clean aromas of apple, pear, and citrus dominate.

**Mouth** Our blind tasters loved the acidity, which lifts the wine above the horde of mediocre Italian whites.

**Design** They're clearly running with this princess theme. One could even go as far as to call it Rococo idiocy. This is a contender for ugliest bottle in the entire book.

# Quinta da Aveleda Vinho Verde

$9

*Two-time Wine Trials selection*

**Style** Light Old World white
**Country** Portugal  **Vintage tasted** 2009
**Grapes** Alvarinho, Loureiro, Trajadura
**Drink with** picnics, fresh caught river fish
**Website** www.aveleda.pt

Rather than spending exorbitant sums on new oak barrels or seeking intensely ripe flavors, most inexpensive Portuguese wines are content to be simple, delicious enhancements to a meal. Whites in particular tend to be light and fresh, recalling flowers and wet stones rather than aggressively fruity, chemical concoctions. Aveleda, which produces many of our favorite Portuguese wines, has mastered this art.

**Nose** It's pretty (though a bit faint), with apple, citrus, and stone.

**Mouth** Lemon, lime, a refreshingly chalky minerality, and blistering acidity make this a great choice with food or by itself on a hot day.

**Design** We abolustely love it—between classy imagery, wonderfully evocative sans-serif fontage, and a sepia color scheme that beautifully matches the color of the wine within, this bottle has the best design-to-dollar ratio of any in the book.

# Quinta da Cabriz

**$11**

Colheita Seleccionada • *Two-time Wine Trials selection*

**Style** Heavy Old World red
**Country** Portugal  **Vintage tasted** 2008
**Grapes** Touriga Nacional, Alfrocheiro, Tinta Roriz
**Drink with** grilled steak, rack of lamb
**Website** www.daosul.com

The Dão region of Portugal is often said to be that country's Burgundy. The wines are made mostly by small farmers rather than huge conglomerates, and the style is usually restrained, elegant, and distinctly food-friendly…right up our alley. Even more than last year's (also excellent) offering, this year's vintage lives up to the region's reputation. Our blind tasters loved its earthiness and barnyard aromas, and they quickly started craving a good steak to accompany the wine.

**Nose** There's rich fruit and earth here. One taster said simply said it smells expensive.

**Mouth** More fruit, along with barnyard flavors and enough acidity to help it pair well with food. We wouldn't necessarily drink it solo, but with dinner it should be superb.

**Design** The drawing seems like it was done by a decently talented child. The raised glass is a nice touch, though.

# Quinta da Romeira

Bucelas DOC, Companhia das Quintas

**Style** Light Old World white
**Country** Portugal  **Vintage tasted** 2008
**Grapes** Arinto
**Drink with** mixed greens, fresh young cheeses
**Website** www.companhiadasquintas.com

Quinta da Romeira is a guesthouse as well as a working winery. This kind of agro-tourism is increasingly popular, especially in Europe, and we're definitely fans—what better way to unwind than by surrounding oneself with growing vines and fermenting wine? We'd love to spend our time getting to better understand how this light, delicious white is made.

**Nose** It's extremely faint, but there are some delicate citrus notes to be found.

**Mouth** It's fruity and light, with continuing citrus and refreshing acidity.

**Design** Nice colors. The scheme is earthy and relaxing. The straw color of the wine and the green hue of the neck foil work splendidly together. But the tacky font and label shape brings it all down.

# René Barbier Mediterranean Red

Catalunya DO • *Two-time Wine Trials selection*

**Style** Light Old World red
**Country** Spain  **Vintage tasted** Non-Vintage
**Grapes** Tempranillo, Garnacha, Monastrell
**Drink with** hamburgers, white pizza
**Website** www.renebarbier.com

There are few things better in the world of wine than the taste of a well aged red. So our blind tasters were thrilled that this impressively cheap bottle had the funky, earthy, herbal notes that typically accompany much older, more expensive wines. This wine is non-vintage, so it's impossible to know exactly how well-aged it actually was—or whether the next bottle will have as many years on it. But at $6, it's definitely worth taking the chance.

**Nose** Our blind tasters called it pretty, and admired the dense, funky, earthy aromas.

**Mouth** The earthy, vegetal notes continue, balanced by some sour cherry. It's big, but smooth.

**Design** It's clearly cheap, but we have to admit the blatant tug on our Mediterranean memories works perfectly.

# René Barbier Mediterranean White $6

Catalunya DO • *Two-time Wine Trials selection*

**Style** Light Old World white
**Country** Spain  **Vintage tasted** Non-Vintage
**Grapes** Xarel-lo, Macabeo, Parellada
**Drink with** cheese spreads, bruschetta
**Website** www.renebarbier.com

With both of its red and white wines included, René Barbier is two for two this year. This wine is particularly impressive for its price: while it showed Champagne-like characteristics last year, this year it managed to pump up its fruit flavors without losing its deliciously fresh, acidic character. And while you won't impress anyone as a big spender, you can win points by rattling off the three grapes in this Catalan wine—Xarel-lo, Macabeo, and Parellada. These also happen to be the classic grapes used to make sparkling Cava.

**Nose** It's simple and refreshing, with aromas of tropical fruit.

**Mouth** It's light, fruity, and acidic. None of our tasters were prepared to write odes to it, but at this price that's just fine.

**Design** The lone seaside chair and sunset have nostalgic meaning for Robin: this was the wine with which his high school friend Meg taught him to drink—and to live well.

# Robert Mondavi Pinot Noir

**$11**

Private Selection • *Three-time Wine Trials selection*

**Style** Light New World red
**Country** USA (CA)  **Vintage tasted** 2008
**Grapes** Pinot Noir, Syrah, Petite Sirah
**Drink with** grilled chicken, roasted vegetables
**Website** www.robertmondavi.com

To some, Robert Mondavi was a viticultural hero who demonstrated California's potential and ushered in a bold new era of powerful, exciting wines; to others, he was a ruthless businessman who helped erase stylistic idiosyncrasies in the wine world. Regardless, this three-time *Wine Trials* selection is stuffed with the aggressive flavors that made Mondavi's reputation.

**Nose** It's a fairly aggressive Pinot Noir nose, with a slight sulfur note that bothered some of our blind tasters.

**Mouth** It evens out considerably here, developing impressive balance. There's also a pleasant vanilla flavor.

**Design** Don't cheapen good wine with bad labels. Do away with the Italianate Mondavi villa shrouded in clouds and the silly-looking calligraphy.

# Root: 1 Sauvignon Blanc

$13

Casablanca Valley

**Style** Light New World white
**Country** Chile  **Vintage tasted** 2009
**Grapes** Sauvignon Blanc
**Drink with** baked fish, fresh green beans
**Website** www.root1wine.com

The folks at Root: 1 have a great hook: they can brag that unlike the vast majority of the world's vines, theirs have ungrafted rootstock. A bit of history: in the late 19th century a plague of small aphid-like insects known as Phylloxera swept across Europe, destroying the roots of most of the grapevines. American vines were resistant, so from then onwards European varieties were grafted onto American rootstock. Some Chilean vineyards, primarily because of their sandy soils, but also because of certain quirks of climate, were unaffected and didn't need to graft. Root: 1 is one such vineyard.

**Nose** Distinctly vegetal aromas are balanced by a hint of fruit.

**Mouth** There's that Sauv Blanc grassiness, along with wonderfully clean acid.

**Design** Eminently cool, it manages to explain the value of ungrafted roots while looking snazzy. And that tree isn't bad, either.

# Rosemount Shiraz

**$10**

Diamond Label • *Three-time Wine Trials selection*

**Style** Heavy New World red
**Country** Australia  **Vintage tasted** 2008
**Grapes** Shiraz
**Drink with** burgers, beef stew
**Website** www.rosemountestateusa.com

Australian Shiraz has been massively popular in the U.S. wine market for some time now. While we feel that this won't hold forever, if and when the fad passes, there will still be plenty of very decent inexpensive wine to be had for the drinker who's willing to disregard the trends of the day. For now, this wine isn't a bad place to start, with its aggressive but not overwhelming flavors and bright fruit.

**Nose** Cherries and a green, vegetal aroma dominate the nose.

**Mouth** It's quite balanced for a Shiraz, with a nice earthy note.

**Design** This diamond motif is really working for them—the combination of the angular bottle and diamond shaped label seem edgy rather than gimmicky.

# Ruffino Chianti

Chianti DOCG

**$12**

**FINALIST**

**Style** Light Old World red
**Country** Italy  **Vintage tasted** 2008
**Grapes** Sangiovese, Canaiolo, Colorino
**Drink with** spaghetti alla bolognese, T-bone steak
**Website** www.ruffino.com

For this wine, third time's the charm. In previous years, our blind tasters found this wine too barnyardy to be appealing, but this year it was just right. An alluring richness and berry flavor balance the earthiness and mulch that are part of most good Chianti wines. We'd be happy to drink this with simple, rustic Italian food any day.

**Nose** It's rich, with a mulchy earthiness that our blind tasters found appealing.

**Mouth** A bright burst of fruit and solid acid provide excellent balance.

**Design** This packaging is all business. No outside marketing experts, no focus groups. The label exists solely to convey the cold, hard facts, and to subject viewers to another ugly crest. And the unusual bottle shape conveys cheapness. This is one case in which progress would definitely be a good thing.

# Ruffino Chianti Superiore

Chianti Superiore DOCG

 $13

**Style** Light Old World red
**Country** Italy  **Vintage tasted** 2007
**Grapes** Sangiovese, Canaiolo, Cabernet Sauvignon, Merlot
**Drink with** wild boar sausage, beef with mushrooms
**Website** www.ruffino.com

Ruffino is one of the largest, and certainly the best known, of the big Chianti producers. You'll find their bottles (which span every price point) at every mid-scale Italian restaurant in the country, and plenty of upper-end joints as well. Those labelled Chianti Superiore are subject to stricter aging requirements—a minimum of nine months, including three months in the bottle—than the base-level Chianti DOCG wines.

**Nose** The rich aromas include earth, vegetables, and mushrooms.

**Mouth** With this wine's distinct taste of autumn leaves and dried tea leaves, it's no wonder one blind taster exclaimed that he could have kept drinking it for a while.

**Design** We like the dark red color scheme, but the sketch of the angel seems a bit much: it's sort of a holy critter wine. At least the extra dollar buys you a more elegant design than Ruffino's entry-level Chianti.

# Ruffino Lumina

Venezia Giulia IGT

**Style** Light Old World white
**Country** Italy  **Vintage tasted** 2009
**Grapes** Pinot Grigio
**Drink with** insalata caprese, grilled white fish
**Website** www.ruffino.com

This is Ruffino's first Pinot Grigio and its first wine produced outside Tuscany—more evidence of Ruffino's solidification as an international powerhouse. This wine is a nice addition to the ever-expanding portfolio. It's light and refreshing, and it has been selling nearly a million bottles a year in the few years it's been produced. Sometimes the masses are right.

**Nose** As one might expect from a Pinot Grigio, it's faint and subtly floral.

**Mouth** Simple and tart, it has a refreshing, chalky aspect that our blind tasters enjoyed.

**Design** We had mixed feelings about the design until we learned that the central icon was the ancient alchemists' symbol for the moon. Now we're all for it. This is by far Ruffino's best-designed bottle

# Samos Muscat

Kourtaki • *Two-time Wine Trials selection*

**Style** Sweet Old World white
**Country** Greece   **Vintage tasted** Non-Vintage
**Grapes** Muscat
**Drink with** blue cheese and honey, roasted nuts

The deep golden color and lovely viscosity of this dessert wine are just part of what makes it a great way to end the night. Honeyed flavors and a rich thickness are the dominating characteristics of this emblematic dessert wine. What's more, it's made on the island of Samos in the Aegean Sea—that ought to impress your dinner guests.

**Nose** The wonderfully honeyed aromas keep coming. Our blind tasters picked up on everything from caramel to raisins.

**Mouth** It's lusciously oily with a nuttiness not unlike you find in some sherries. There's a bit of sweet honeysuckle there, too.

**Design** There's an interesting monochromatic effect from the similarities between the gold label and the color of the wine; for that, we'll forgive the rest.

# San Lorenzo Chianti

Chianti DOCG • *Two-time Wine Trials selection*

**Style** Light Old World red
**Country** Italy  **Vintage tasted** 2008
**Grapes** Sangiovese, Sanvgiovese Grosso
**Drink with** your favorite Italian-American comfort dishes

San Lorenzo is the patron saint of librarians, roasters, and butchers. He suffered one of the most distinctive martyrdoms in history: he is said to have been martyred on a gridiron (grill) as part of Valerian's persecution. During his barbecue, he cried out "This side's done, turn me over and have a bite." Not only does that explain the whole butcher/roaster thing, it makes him a clear ancestor of the James Bonds and Bruce Willises of the world. None of which says much about the wine, but come on, how could we pass up that story?

**Nose** Classic Chianti aromas of crushed red berries, forest floor, earth, and herbs abound.

**Mouth** Savory in flavor and sleek and slightly acidic in feel, this wine is an ideal accompaniment to tomato-heavy Italian food.

**Design** Red and gold foil, with aristocratic fonts: there's nothing wrong, per se, but it's getting a bit old.

# Santa Ema Chardonnay

**$10**

Casablanca Valley • *Two-time Wine Trials selection*

**Style** Heavy New World white
**Country** Chile  **Vintage tasted** 2009
**Grapes** Chardonnay
**Drink with** fish and chips, fried chicken
**Website** www.santaema.cl

Chile, like Argentina, is thought of by many bargain-conscious consumers as an "it" region. It makes sense that wines coming from South America would be cheaper than their counterparts in California; land costs less, as does labor, among other things. And as far as Chardonnay goes, the Casablanca Valley is a cool climate, ensuring that the wines aren't big, knock-you-over-the-head specimens. See—the stars have aligned to produce cheap Chards like this one.

**Nose** With tons of mineral and definite oak, this wine has a few of the Chardonnay bases covered.

**Mouth** More oak, but it's not overpowering. Some of our blind tasters also detected a slight prickle.

**Design** The golden-wine-against-red-label color scheme works, but there's a bit too much gilded edge going on around the nameplate. Still, it's reasonably elegant and inoffensive, looking neither cheap nor expensive.

# Santa Ema Sauvignon Blanc

(\$10)

Maipo Valley • *Two-time Wine Trials selection*

**Style** Light New World white
**Country** Chile  **Vintage tasted** 2009
**Grapes** Sauvignon Blanc
**Drink with** mozzarella and tomato sandwich, artichokes
**Website** www.santaema.cl

Santa Ema proudly broadcasts its status as a mega-winery: it's one of the largest Chilean wineries, it exports to more than 30 countries, and it's reliably one of the top 10 sellers in the US. None of which would give us much confidence in the actual quality of the wine if it weren't for the fact that Santa Ema turns out consistent winners. For two years in a row, both the Chardonnay and Sauvignon Blanc have been hits with our blind tasters, proving that it's possible to be the biggest and one of the best, too.

**Nose** Those grassy, cabbagey aromas mark it as a Sauv Blanc from miles away.

**Mouth** There's tons of tart acidity, along with continuing vegetal flavors—very classic and very delicious.

**Design** The green label against the pale, straw-colored wine is a nice effect. But the gold is a tacky touch to an otherwise classy bottle.

# Santa Julia Cabernet Sauvignon

Mendoza • *Two-time Wine Trials selection*

**Style** Heavy New World red
**Country** Argentina  **Vintage tasted** 2009
**Grapes** Cabernet Sauvignon
**Drink with** carne asada, grilled mushrooms
**Website** www.familiazuccardi.com

Many critics of organic winemaking hint that organic mass producers can't achieve reliable, consistent quality without the aids of pesticides and other chemicals. But the continuingly high quality of this Cabernet (it's been selected by our blind tasters two years running) suggests that Argentina's Familia Zuccardi has found a way to combine consistency, delicious wine, organic methods, and low prices. Sounds about right to us.

**Nose** The crushed fruit and ripe berries are countered by the green pepper and other vegetal aromas.

**Mouth** Our blind tasters found it a bit green and suggested it could use a few more months before being drunk. But they were still impressed with the balance.

**Design** Simple and sleek, this bottle looks like it should be on the wall of a trendy Manhattan apartment.

# Santa Julia Malbec

Mendoza, Familia Zuccardi

**Style** Heavy New World red
**Country** Argentina **Vintage tasted** 2009
**Grapes** Malbec
**Drink with** Argentine steaks, grilled mushrooms
**Website** www.familiazuccardi.com

It's hard not to like the sentiment behind proudly organic growers, even if they can occasionally seem preachy, and this eco-friendly Argentine winery turns out a fruity but complex wine that's delicious. Like several of our picks from South America, this wine expertly walks the line between New World and Old World styles, with berries and a nice herbaceous quality.

**Nose** Berry and grape aromas dominate (yes, we know—all wines may be made of grapes, but not all wines smell like them). There's also a nice herbal note that lends this bottle some Old World class.

**Mouth** Big red berries, herbs, and a healthy dose of food-friendly acid appealed instantly to our blind tasters.

**Design** The unusually shaped label and simple black-and-white design make this bottle seem more expensive than it is—though we could have lived without the statue of a woman's head.

# Sebeka Chenin Blanc
Western Cape

**Style** Aromatic New World white
**Country** South Africa  **Vintage tasted** 2008
**Grapes** Chenin Blanc
**Drink with** Indian curries, dosai
**Website** www.sebekawines.com

The description on the back of this South African bottle suggests that the vineyards are constantly being visited (and possibly tended to) by majestic cheetahs. While we doubt that's the case, we were huge fans of this mineral-driven wine. Chenin Blanc is Africa's signature white grape, and it's easy to see why: its slight sweetness is balanced by substantial acidity, and its bright flavors are impossible to resist.

**Nose** Our blind tasters picked out the aromas of grass, minerals, and even lemon Pine-Sol.

**Mouth** The sensation of clean, wet rock persists here, accompanied by a slight sweetness.

**Design** The blurred background gives an indication of the cheetah's speed. He must be running late to his majestic visit to the grapes.

# Seven Daughters Winemakers Blend

**$15**

**Style** Heavy New World red **Country** USA (CA)
**Vintage tasted** Non-Vintage **Grapes** Merlot, Cabernet Franc,
Cabernet Sauvignon, Zinfandel, Syrah, Carignan, Sangiovese
**Drink with** pork chops, boiled cabbage
**Website** www.7daughters.com

Seven Daughters takes its name from the seven grapes that go into this blend. And while we have a sneaking suspicion that some of the grapes were added just to reach the magic number (we doubt the winemaker actually thought to himself, "what this wine needs is Carignan"), the resulting blend is thoroughly delicious.

**Nose** It's packed with powerful aromas of fruit, smoke, and eucalyptus.

**Mouth** Cherry dominates. It's big but not particularly tannic.

**Design** Perhaps the best-designed label in *The Wine Trials 2011*, this masterwork manages to mingle the simplicity of Swiss fontage, a harmonious color wheel (representing the seven grape varieties) that's evocative of late-20th-century modernism, and a design-school use of negative space. This masterpiece is worth the $15 for the bottle alone. (If you don't pay attention to the clichéd text, that is.)

# Snoqualmie Whistle Stop Red

Columbia Valley

**$10**

**Style** Heavy New World red
**Country** USA (WA) **Vintage tasted** 2007
**Grapes** Cabernet Sauvignon, Merlot
**Drink with** burgers, pulled pork
**Website** www.snoqualmie.com

We're always pleased when sustainable vintners produce great wines, and this is definitely one of those. It's a Bordeaux blend (Cabernet and Merlot) with the extra layers of fruit you'd expect in a New World wine. But the healthy tannins and acid create impressive balance, and you don't have to be a fan of the New World style to enjoy this impressive effort.

**Nose** There's plenty of red and black fruit here, but it's surprisingly restrained, all things considered.

**Mouth** More dark fruit, and one blind taster picked up a hint of chocolate. It's definitely tannic, so be prepared with a juicy steak.

**Design** Very cool, very Pacific Northwest. It almost looks as if the original medium was chalk on paper, giving this a hip feel without being the least bit gimmicky. The font, however, is hideous.

# Starborough Sauvignon Blanc

($13)

Marlborough

**Style** Light New World white
**Country** New Zealand  **Vintage tasted** 2008
**Grapes** Sauvignon Blanc
**Drink with** baked goat cheese, raw oysters
**Website** www.starboroughwines.com

This was a favorite Sauvignon Blanc with many tasters, so if you enjoy the distinct flavors and aromas of this grape, New Zealand style, we recommend you grab a bottle. It nicely balances fruit and citrus flavors with the green, vegetal flavors that often distinguish Sauvignon Blanc. Bring on the hot sun and summer days.

**Nose** Our blind tasters loved the clean aromas of melon and apple cider, as well as the biting cabbage note.

**Mouth** It's beautifully balanced, with candied lemon and other citrus flavors.

**Design** The star looks quite aquatic, rather like a starfish. But the vines are squarely in the realm of the terrestrial. Nonetheless, it's a very fun and cheery bottle.

# Steakhouse Red

 **$13**

**Style** Heavy New World red
**Country** USA (WA) **Vintage tasted** 2008
**Grapes** Cabernet Sauvignon
**Drink with** a steak, obviously
**Website** www.magnificentwine.com

This cousin to the ever popular House Wine is the beefier, gruffer member of the family. While it has some of the same fruit flavors as House Wine, Steakhouse is dominated by herbal and vegetal flavors that can take a bit to warm up to—but that come into their own when paired with (you guessed it) a great steak. We certainly wouldn't recommend sipping it solo, though; depending on which of our blind tasters you ask, you'll think you've been drinking earth, pine trees, or asparagus.

**Nose** Our blind tasters mentioned overpowering green pepper, black fruit, and herbs.

**Mouth** It's astringent and tannic, with pine, mint, and a bit of fruit.

**Design** We're still not fans of this 6-year-old's-handwriting font, and we certainly can't imagine this bottle being opened at a reputable steakhouse. Whatever happened to truth in advertising?

# Targovishte Riesling

LVK Vinprom

$9

**Style** Aromatic Old World white
**Country** Bulgaria  **Vintage tasted** 2009
**Grapes** Riesling
**Drink with** Buffalo chicken wings, chicken in white wine
**Website** www.lvk-vinprom.com

Riesling is one of the grapes most sensitive to terroir (the combination of soil, weather, and general sense of place). So it's always interesting to try a Riesling from a new area—especially when that area is as unusual as Bulgaria. And while this wine didn't knock us out with exotic flavors and aromas, it did provide a surprisingly strong example of a good, enjoyable Riesling.

**Nose** It's honeyed and floral, with citrus and even some peach—our blind tasters were impressed.

**Mouth** It's fairly sweet but not overpoweringly so, with a long, floral finish.

**Design** Challenge to readers: if you can find an uglier bottle than this great-aunt's-house-china-closet ridged-glass monstrosity, send us a picture of it and we'll send you a free book. But we have to agree that it's uglier. Which is not likely.

# Targovishte Sauvignon Blanc

**LVK Vinprom**

**Style** Light Old World white
**Country** Bulgaria  **Vintage tasted** 2009
**Grapes** Sauvignon Blanc
**Drink with** goat cheese and tomato sandwich, summer picnics
**Website** www.lvk-vinprom.com

Whether it's from New Zealand, California, or Bulgaria, there are a few things we always look for in a Sauvignon Blanc: bright flavors and aromas (preferably with a good balance between fruit and grassiness), food-friendliness, and tons of refreshing acidity. This bottle is three for three, with intense citrus and tropical fruit aromas that remind us of a New Zealand Sauv Blanc and enough acidity to melt metal. We couldn't be happier, and we'll definitely keep an eye open for other Bulgarian Sauv Blancs in the future.

**Nose** Tropical fruit, bright citrus, green apple, and floral aromas thrilled our blind tasters.

**Mouth** More of the same here, along with blistering acidity that will make this wine a hit on a hot day.

**Design** This is the most disgustingly ugly bottle we've ever laid eyes on. Actually—scratch that, it's a tie: there's one other Targovishte in *The Wine Trials 2011.*

# 35° South Sauvignon Blanc

Viña San Pedro • *Three-time Wine Trials selection*

**$9**

FINALIST

**Style** Light New World white
**Country** Chile  **Vintage tasted** 2009
**Grapes** Sauvignon Blanc
**Drink with** artichoke salad, grilled shrimp
**Website** www.sanpedro.cl

The Southern Hemisphere's 35th parallel isn't a bad place to grow grapes, especially, it seems, Sauvignon Blanc: this wine has been a *Wine Trials* selection three years running. It possesses that "cat pee" smell that so characterizes the grape. It's a repulsive image, but the description works; otherwise, we can't think of a better way to describe the aromas than, "uh, smells like Sauvignon Blanc." We've heard it described as boxwood bud, but since we're not sure what that is, we'll have to stick with cat pee.

**Nose** It's incredibly green, with aromas of vegetables and grass.

**Mouth** Bracingly acidic and vegetal—one blind taster said it tasted like drinking pickle juice.

**Design** The label manages to pull off a navigational theme, borrowing from the look of old maps, without coming off as too precious or gimmicky. But the big colored "S" in the middle of the logo ruins everything.

# Toasted Head Cabernet Sauvignon

North Coast

**Style** Heavy New World red
**Country** USA (CA) **Vintage tasted** 2007
**Grapes** Cabernet Sauvignon, Petit Verdot
**Drink with** steak, itself
**Website** www.toastedhead.com

This is a Cab in the classic California jammy style—and we couldn't help but love it. It's easy to write off this ubiquitous, cutesy bottle when you see it on a grocery shelf, but it handily won our tasters over in blind tastings. The rich fruit and bold tannins are tough to hate, and if you're a fan of New World reds, you'll go nuts. And feel free to put it in a brown paper bag before drinking.

**Nose** Our blind tasters noticed strong dark berries, prunes, and even a hint of chocolate.

**Mouth** It's rich and expansive, with a definite hit of California tannin.

**Design** Well, it's a critter wine, but this critter breathes fire. Still, the font, color scheme, label shape, and use of space make up for our inherent anti-critter leanings. If you're going to go critter, this is the way to do it.

# Trivento Reserve Malbec
Mendoza

$12

**Style** Heavy New World red
**Country** Argentina  **Vintage tasted** 2008
**Grapes** Malbec
**Drink with** sweetbreads, sirloin
**Website** www.trivento.com

Trivento's website proclaims that "three winds rush over Mendoza land, leaving their mark in all of our wines." Unfortunately, we're still left with the burning question of who came up with that awful phrase. Their wine is significantly better than their advertising, thankfully. This bottle is herbal, fruity, and perfectly balanced—so maybe there is something to all that wind stuff.

**Nose** It's distinctly herbal and complex, with an interesting aroma that is a bit chemical.

**Mouth** There are herbs and red fruit and a balanced, medium body. The finish is nice and long.

**Design** Presumably, the font of "Trivento" is trying, once again, to convey the idea of three winds (the three letters with wind-brushed tails, the two "T"s and the "R"), and once again, it manages to be done in the tackiest possible way. Thankfully, the use of space and a decent color scheme make up for it.

# Trivento Reserve Torrontés
Mendoza

**$12**

**FINALIST**

**Style** Aromatic New World white
**Country** Argentina  **Vintage tasted** 2009
**Grapes** Torrontés
**Drink with** hard aged cheese, melon
**Website** www.trivento.com

Torrontés has carved a niche for itself as the signature white grape of Argentina, and the fresh, floral, aromatic wines it produces seem perfectly suited to the American market. It may not have much name recognition in the mass market yet, but we wouldn't be surprised if it eventually became as ubiquitous as Sauvignon Blanc. Wines like this one—flowery but fresh—make us excited for the day you'll find mini-bottles of Torrontés on your JetBlue flight to Buffalo.

**Nose** Flowers and peaches are the most obvious of the many notes in this aromatic wine.

**Mouth** There's florality here as well, along with more fruit and a slight herbal quality. It's all very refreshing.

**Design** Those metallic colors and awful green color make it look a bit cheap; we'd prefer a slightly classier look for a "reserve" wine at this price.

# Turning Leaf Pinot Noir
Provincia di Pavia IGT

**Style** Light Old World red
**Country** Italy **Vintage tasted** 2007
**Grapes** Pinot Noir
**Drink with** seared duck breast, chicken salad
**Website** www.turningleaf.com

An $8 Pinot Noir that's both mass produced and delicious? We wouldn't have believed it either, until we blind tasted it. Pinot Noir is a grape that tends to fall into sharp stylistic camps: the New World profile of ripe cherries with some earth against the Old World model of barnyard, earth, nuts, and a bit of red fruit to balance it all out. This wine is impressively complex and definitely tends towards the Old World. Our blind tasters were pleasantly surprised by the price tag.

**Nose** It smells of hazelnut, wood, and fresh tomato vine—all in all, an incredibly appealing mixture.

**Mouth** It's more nutty than fruity, and it also has tomato and loads of spicy black pepper.

**Design** We can't put our finger on exactly what bothers us about this label. Perhaps all that gold leaf just seems a little too perfect. Either way, it's hard to complain given how distinctive the wine inside is.

# Umani Ronchi Sangiovese
Marche IGT

**Style** Heavy Old World red
**Country** Italy  **Vintage tasted** 2008
**Grapes** Sangiovese
**Drink with** wild boar ragù, prosciutto
**Website** www.umanironchi.com

Sangiovese is the grape behind the great wines of Chianti, Brunello di Montalcino, as well as this wine— and judging by the exclamation point on this bottle, the folks at Umani Ronchi are awfully excited about it. We can see why: it has the classic mix of earth and fruit flavors that makes many Italian wines so appealing. If you hate the smell of farms or forests, you should probably stay away.

**Nose** There's lots of ripe fruit here, along with earthy aromas that made one blind taster think of forest floor.

**Mouth** It starts off full and fruity, but quickly adds flavors of earth, undergrowth, and what one taster identified as an animal byproduct we'll euphemistically call barnyard. But trust us, it's great.

**Design** The theme is a bit overplayed, with the punctuation mark appearing both on the bottle and on the neck. But we do like the simple sans serif font, and the fact that there aren't too many words

# Valleclaro Rosado

Vinos Sin Ley

**Style** Rosé
**Country** Spain **Vintage tasted** 2009
**Grapes** Prieto Picudo
**Drink with** arroz con pollo, fresh crab

In an effort to promote innovative winemaking, a group of vintners from around Spain banded together to produce wines that depart from the traditions of Spanish winemaking. They call themselves Vinos Sin Ley. Their techniques often violate the strict wine production laws of the state as well, and they wear this fact as a badge of pride: Vinos Sin Ley translates into "wines without law."

**Nose** No one was impressed with its unnatural hot pink color, but the rich fruity nose prompted several tasters to compare it to an intense red wine.

**Mouth** One blind taster was reminded of rhubarb and cherry pie…à la mode. Since that's certainly not like any Spanish wine we've ever tasted before, this whole without-laws thing must be doing something.

**Design** The color scheme here is incredibly funky; this bottle would be right at a home on the wall of an artsy California boutique.

# Vieux Papes Blanc de Blancs

**Style** Light Old World white
**Country** France **Vintage tasted** Non-Vintage
**Grapes** Ugni Blanc, Sauvignon Blanc, Chardonnay
**Drink with** beet salad, stir fried vegetables
**Website** www.vieuxpapes.com

This wine left our tasters confused. Many of them noted that it tasted like a Sauvignon Blanc, but there was something strange about it. We discovered what that was when we pulled off the brown paper bag: the Sauvignon Blanc (which is normally made solo or perhaps with Sémillon) was blended with Chardonnay and Ugni Blanc. It's all made weirder by the fact that Blanc de Blancs is a term reserved for sparkling wines made exclusively from the Chardonnay grape.

**Nose** It's got nice minerality, along with peach and floral aromas from the other grapes. One of our blind tasters detected a slight chemical note.

**Mouth** Orange, lime, and citrus flavors mingle wonderfully. There's even enough acid to cut through all that fruit.

**Design** That script is a bold play, but it seems to work. We hope it doesn't start a trend, though: things could go wrong very quickly.

# Vieux Papes Rouge

**Style** Light Old World red
**Country** France  **Vintage tasted** Non-Vintage
**Grapes** Carignan, Cabernet Sauvignon, Merlot
**Drink with** ham and baguette, beef kebab
**Website** www.vieuxpapes.com

Castel Frères is the largest owner and winemaker in Bordeaux, with fourteen different châteaux. This is not, from our perspective, anything to brag about—quantity is rarely related to quality in the wine world. But between all of those vineyards, some of the wines turn out to be truly delicious, such as this classic Old World table wine. It's unassuming and subtle, with just enough flavor to stand up to food.

**Nose** It's fairly faint, but there is an Old World vibe that our blind tasters enjoyed.

**Mouth** Extremely simple (the better to pair with a wide variety of dishes), it's quite sleek in the mouth. It has definite acidity as well as tannins that are almost nonexistent.

**Design** It's making a definite play at looking like classy French table wine—and it works for us. The script somehow even manages to be charming rather than froofy.

# Villa Maria Sauvignon Blanc

Marlborough • *Three-time Wine Trials selection*

**Style** Light New World white
**Country** New Zealand  **Vintage tasted** 2009
**Grapes** Sauvignon Blanc
**Drink with** whole roasted fish, shrimp cocktail
**Website** www.villamaria.co.nz

Despite a name that's about as evocative of New Zealand as a tortilla, this wine is, for the second year in a row, a classic Kiwi concoction. We are also impressed with the makers' unabashed commitment to screwtops: Villa Maria, to achieve better consistency, was the first maker in the world to declare its winery a "cork-free zone."

**Nose** It's almost a parody of the style: candied and tropical fruits, flowers, and vegetal aromas combine into an aggressive nose.

**Mouth** It's a bit less intense here, with tropical fruit, floral flavors, and refreshing acidity.

**Design** There's really no excuse for a New World winery founded in 1961 to use a coat of arms. We wish Villa Maria would cut out the faux-aristocratic red and gold and create a bottle that reflects the fun, lively wine inside.

# Villa Wolf Dry Riesling

Pfalz

**Style** Aromatic Old World white
**Country** Germany  **Vintage tasted** 2008
**Grapes** Riesling
**Drink with** pork chops, ceviche
**Website** www.jlwolf.com

We're thrilled to see some dry Rieslings make it into this year's edition of *The Wine Trials*; this style can be difficult to adjust to, so it's nice to see the market slowly starting to embrace it so wholeheartedly. To be fair, this bottle wasn't completely dry: several of our blind tasters detected a hit of sugar before the intense acidity washed away any sweetness. Given how bracing great dry Riesling can be, this seems like a fair compromise to us.

**Nose** It's got a classically aromatic Riesling nose, with clean minerality and citrus.

**Mouth** Any sweetness is quickly forgotten in the sharp attack of acidity and minerality.

**Design** This isn't a traditional German label. In fact, it's quite ugly, especially the Wolf logo against the blue. It reminds us of a White House State Dinner invitation.

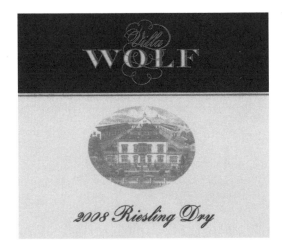

# Villa Wolf Pinot Gris

Pfalz

**Style** Light Old World white
**Country** Germany  **Vintage tasted** 2007
**Grapes** Pinot Gris
**Drink with** baked clams, white fish
**Website** www.jlwolf.com

Yes, Pinot Gris is the same grape as Pinot Grigio, but the choice of the Francophone name often signals a more restrained style. This one is certainly true to type, with floral aromas and great balance. It comes from the Pfalz region of Germany (as does the Pölka Dot Riesling), though it lacks some of the acidity that makes many German wines so exciting.

**Nose** It's faint (we'd say restrained) and floral.

**Mouth** It's almost prickly in the mouth, with peach and lemon flavors and mouthwatering acid.

**Design** With frills and garbage script fonts everywhere, this label is a total abuse of some computer design program. It's not classic in any way.

# Viña Los Vascos Sauvignon Blanc  $11
Casablanca Valley

**Style** Light New World white
**Country** Chile  **Vintage tasted** 2009
**Grapes** Sauvignon Blanc
**Drink with** stuffed grape leaves, pasta salad
**Website** www.lafite.com

We've frequently found that Chilean wines walk the thin line between Old World and New World styles, and this Sauvignon Blanc is no exception—not surprising, given the fact that Los Vascos is part of the Lafite group. It has the grassy, vegetal quality of New Zealand Sauv Blancs as well as the fruitier notes found in top cold-climate examples. It has enough of those classic aromas to let most of our blind tasters know that this is mostly definitely a Sauvignon Blanc.

**Nose** Tropical fruit, cat pee, and vegetables: sounds like a Sauvignon Blanc to us.

**Mouth** One blind taster called it bright, grassy, and acidic; it also has a nice herbal quality that's hard to dislike.

**Design** It's one of the classiest examples of the vineyard-sketch label we've seen. The simple shading, nicely done drawing, and well chosen fonts make this a study in label making.

# Vinha da Defesa

Herdade do Esporão, Alentejo

**Style** Light Old World white
**Country** Portugal  **Vintage tasted** 2008
**Grapes** Arinto, Roupeiro, Antão Vaz
**Drink with** picnics, fresh crab
**Website** www.esporao.com

Good luck keeping track of the grapes in Portuguese wines; there are more of them than we've ever been able to remember. This wine is made up of Arinto, Roupeiro, and Antão Vaz, which we're pretty sure translate into "delicious," "inexpensive," and "balanced," respectively. In any case, this bottle is precisely what we look for in a Portuguese wine: subtle and understated, it's a perfect table wine at a price that doesn't require special occasions.

**Nose** There are green apples, flowers (one blind taster picked out lavender), and a slight grassiness.

**Mouth** It's crisp, understated, and clean, with bright flavors of apple and a solid body.

**Design** It's sleek, futuristic, and just plain cool. We'd love to see more labels done in this simple, semi-transparent style.

# VINI Cabernet Sauvignon
Bulgarian Master Vintners

$8

**Style** Heavy Old World red
**Country** Bulgaria **Vintage tasted** 2008
**Grapes** Cabernet Sauvignon
**Drink with** onion soup, beef stew

When was the last time you had a good Bulgarian Cab? We definitely don't spend much time drinking Bulgarian wine, so we were pleasantly surprised when the brown bag came off this bottle. Fans of juicy New World Cabs might be shocked, though: this wine is a perfect example of what the wine world calls "green" flavors. That is, it's reminiscent of cabbage, asparagus, herbs, grass—take your pick. And while that may not be for everyone, it's certainly worth giving a try.

**Nose** It reminded our blind tasters of green peppers, mulch, and fresh herbs. One taster commented that it seemed to jump out of the glass.

**Mouth** There are more herbal flavors here, with an impressive level of balance.

**Design** Bulgarian chic: it looks like the Russian oligarchs are behind the use of gold and shiny red. Very luxurious, indeed.

## Washington Hills Late Harvest Riesling

Summit Reserve, Columbia Valley

**Style** Sweet New World white
**Country** USA (WA)  **Vintage tasted** 2008
**Grapes** Riesling
**Drink with** really pungent cheeses
**Website** www.washingtonhills.com

Typically, "late harvest" means just what it sounds like: grapes are harvested later than usual, allowing them to further ripen and develop more sugar. This can be more difficult than it sounds. If made without care or with a low-acidity grape, the wine can be sickly and cloying. But when done well, a late harvest wine can offer rich flavors and decadent sweetness, followed by a cleansing swipe of acidity.

**Nose** So delicate it's hard to pick out individual components, the nose definitely has floral aromas, straw, and faint fruit. One blind taster also smelled candle wax.

**Mouth** Many of our blind tasters experienced the same progression: an initial honeyed sweetness (with some peach flavor) quickly gave way to bright acidity.

**Design** This is a beautiful label. The landscape evokes the Pacific Northwest nostalgia within us all.

# Washington Hills Merlot

Columbia Valley

**Style** Light New World red
**Country** USA (WA)  **Vintage tasted** 2008
**Grapes** Merlot, Cabernet Franc
**Drink with** chicken and rice, pulled pork
**Website** www.washingtonhills.com

Ever since *Sideways*, American Merlot has had a bad reputation among many wine drinkers. That's not entirely fair: even cheap domestic Merlot can be ripe and delicious. This example fits squarely in that mold—while it's certainly very ripe, it manages to avoid tasting like fruit juice. So we'll raise a glass to Paul Giamatti; thanks to you, there's more for us.

**Nose** Our blind tasters loved the red fruit, which is matched by the distinct aroma of bell pepper.

**Mouth** Fresh fruit abounds, along with food-friendly acidity and a bit of tannin.

**Design** This simple bottle, with its evocation of the Pacific Northwest mountains, stirs our patriotic pride. The pretty but restrained picture makes for great design.

# Waterbrook Mélange Noir

Columbia Valley

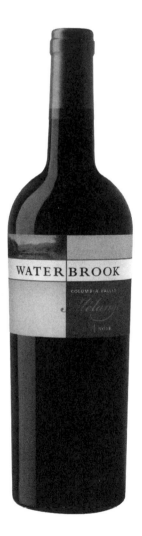

**$15**

**Style** Heavy New World red
**Country** USA (WA)  **Vintage tasted** 2007
**Grapes** Merlot, Cabernet Sauvignon, Sangiovese, Cabernet Franc
**Drink with** pot roast and mashed potatoes
**Website** www.waterbrook.com

When they say this is a mélange, they aren't kidding: the blend includes Merlot, Cabernet Sauvignon, Sangiovese, and Cabernet Franc. It's not often you see the Bordeaux-based Cab Franc with the Italian Sangiovese, but given our blind tasters' reactions, maybe the folks at Waterbrook are on to something. The wine seems to have picked up the best characteristics of its grapes while avoiding their defects, leading to a complex, completely enjoyable end product.

**Nose** Our blind tasters found the nose pleasantly restrained, with a woody smell.

**Mouth** It's savory, with black fruit, mineral, and some nice chewiness.

**Design** The symmetry of the label creates a beautiful effect that would be at home on a much more expensive bottle. And the landscape shows the Washington State we know and love.

# Woodbridge Chardonnay

Robert Mondavi

**$8**

**Style** Heavy New World white
**Country** USA (CA)  **Vintage tasted** 2008
**Grapes** Chardonnay
**Drink with** lemon chicken, seared halibut
**Website** www.robertmondavi.com

Nearly as ubiquitous as Yellow Tail, the Woodbridge label can be found in just about every liquor store in America—and an impressive number of Walgreens, bodegas, and gas stations as well. It's not particularly known for simplicity and elegance, though, which is why our blind tasters were surprised when the brown bag came off this bottle. It's impressively fresh and clean for an American Chardonnay, which makes us like it even more.

**Nose** It's simple and floral, with bright citrus flavors as well.

**Mouth** Again and again, our blind tasters used words like simple, clean, and refreshing. Sounds good to us.

**Design** We've seen it so many times it's hard to form an opinion. On second thought, it's not that hard: it looks like a poorly designed grocery store wine.

# Yalumba Shiraz Viognier

Y Series, South Australia

$10

**Style** Heavy New World red
**Country** Australia  **Vintage tasted** 2008
**Grapes** Shiraz, Viognier
**Drink with** feijoada, lamb tagine
**Website** www.yalumba.com

Yalumba is borrowing from the northern Rhône with this Shiraz-Viognier mix. Producers there have long been permitted to tame Syrah (a powerful, bold red grape) with Viognier (a flowery, aromatic white). Unlike many other blends, these wines are made by mixing the two grape varieties before fermentation, rather than after. Proponents say this preserves a brighter color and adds aromatic properties.

**Nose** Strong vegetal aromas mix with black fruit and molasses.

**Mouth** It's spicy, with rough tannins, some acid, and a burst of fruit. One blind taster called it a "good country wine."

**Design** The bottle is a well-designed screwtop, and we like the simple color scheme. The rampant horse is a bit much, though.

# Yalumba Unwooded Chardonnay

Y Series, South Australia

**Style** Light New World white
**Country** Australia  **Vintage tasted** 2009
**Grapes** Chardonnay
**Drink with** fish tacos, fresh field salad
**Website** www.yalumba.com

Since the anti-oak movement took hold a few years ago, "Unwooded" or "Unoaked" Chardonnay has become a ubiquitous household designation almost entirely associated with Australia—and it's a designation almost always for cheap wines, not expensive ones. And you still almost never see expensive Chardonnays, from Australia or California or anywhere else, that aren't oaky—it's the cheap ones that have moved in the less oaky direction in the past few years. Yalumba's is a stellar example of this trend.

**Nose** With its bright citrus and tropical fruit flavors, it would be easy to mistake this wine for a Sauvignon Blanc.

**Mouth** It manages to be both juicy and crisp, with bright acid to meet the full apple flavors.

**Design** We like the classy lowercase fontage. And that bird is so well drawn that we hesitate to call this a critter wine; we'll give it a pass, for now.

# Zardetto Prosecco

*Two-time Wine Trials selection*

$14

**Style** Sparkling
**Country** Italy  **Vintage tasted** Non-Vintage
**Grapes** Glera, Chardonnay
**Drink with** bagels and lox, smoked herring
**Website** www.zardettoprosecco.com

Prosecco made with Glera? You read that right. In 2009, the name of the grape was changed back to its old moniker to reduce confusion surrounding a newly minted DOCG. So Zardetto Prosecco is indeed Prosecco. Its flavor profile is quite different from that of Champagne; it doesn't have the so-called "creamy mousse" that the wine establishment looks for in French sparklers. Rather, it's light-bodied and fruity, neither yeasty nor toasty—a lot like hard cider, in fact.

**Nose** It's fairly faint. Still, blind tasters smelled red apples and a bit of minerality.

**Mouth** There's more red apple, more crisp acidity. The bubbles are a bit coarse, and some blind tasters complained about the general over-fizziness of this bottle.

**Design** The jarring juxtaposition of two utterly unrelated 1980s-ish fonts is amusing, but hardly harmonious. And do they really need to write "bubbly" all over the foil?

# Appendix Conclusions of the 2008 experiment

By Johan Almenberg and Anna Dreber Almenberg

Contrary to what we might expect, people do not appreciate expensive wines more (when they are unaware of the price). In a sample of more than 6,000 blind tastings, we find that the correlation between price and overall rating is small and *negative*, suggesting that individuals on average enjoy more expensive wines slightly *less*. For people with wine training (hereafter, "experts"), however, we find indications of a positive correlation.

In the regression analysis, the dependent variable is the overall rating, measured on a scale from 1 to 4, with 4 being the highest rating. The price variable is the natural logarithm of the dollar price. (If we didn't do this, we would be expecting a one-dollar increase to have the same effect at the $5 price level as at the $50 price level; this seems counterintuitive. We do get the same qualitative results using the dollar prices, but the statistical significance of the coefficients deteriorates.)

We use an ordered probit estimator as well as a linear estimator (OLS). In both cases we use robust standard errors. The ordered probit estimator is particularly well suited to an ordinal dependent variable, but we find that OLS also performs well, and yields estimates that are easier to interpret. In any case, the two models generate highly consistent results.

We employ three model specifications, and run all three using both the ordered probit and the OLS estimator. In Model 1, we regress the overall rating assigned to wine $i$, by individual $j$, on the price of the wine. In Model 2, we allow for the possibility that wine "experts," such as sommeliers or people with professional wine training, rate wines in a different manner. We include a dummy variable for being an expert, as well as an interaction term for price and the expert dummy. In a linear regression, this allows both the intercept and the slope coefficient to differ for experts and non-experts. In terms of the linear model, we can write these two models as

(1) $y_i = \beta_0 + \beta_1 \ln(PRICE_i) + \varepsilon_i$

and

(2) $y_i = \beta_0 + \beta_1 \ln(PRICE_i) + \beta_2 EXPERT_j + \beta_3 \ln(PRICE_i) * EXPERT_j + \varepsilon_i$

If individuals found that more expensive wine tasted better, the correlation between overall rating and price would be positive. In our sample, this is not the case: the coefficient on price is *negative* regardless of whether we use ordered probit or OLS. The linear estimator offers an interpretation of the magnitude of the effect: when we estimate model 1 using OLS, the coefficient is about -0.04, implying that a 100% increase in the (natural) log of the price is associated with a 0.04 reduction in the overall rating. The negative effect is moderate, but statistically significant ($p$-value: 0.038).

Unlike the non-experts, experts assign as high, or higher, ratings to more expensive wines. The interaction term for price and being an expert is highly statistically significant throughout. Controlling for experts produces a larger negative effect of price for non-experts, with improved statistical significance (ordered probit/OLS $p$-values: 0.013/0.012).

In addition, experts assign overall ratings that are on average half a rating point lower (OLS coefficient on the expert dummy: -0.448, $p$-value < 0.001). Regardless of whether we use ordered probit or OLS, estimation of Model 2 indicates that the correlation between price and overall rating is positive—or, at any rate, non-negative—

for experts. The "net" coefficient for experts is the sum of the coefficient on ln(price) and the coefficient on ln(price)*expert. With OLS, this is approximately 0.1 and marginally statistically significant ($p$-value: 0.09). For ordered probit, the net coefficient is about 0.11 and marginally statistically significant ($p$-value: 0.099). The price coefficient for non-experts is negative.

When we estimate Model 2 using OLS, the model predicts that for a wine that costs ten times more than another wine, if we were to use a 100-point scale (such as that used by *Wine Spectator*), the linear model predicts that for a wine that costs 10 times more than another wine, non-experts will on average assign an overall rating that is about four points *lower*, whereas experts will assign an overall rating that is about seven points *higher*. If the dollar price increases by a factor of 10, ln(price) increases by about 2.3. Hence the predicted effect on the overall rating of tenfold increase in the dollar price is 2.3 times the ln(price) coefficient for non-experts and experts, respectively.

We also test a third model, including individual fixed effects. Model 3 is essentially the same as Model 2, except that we add a dummy variable $j$ for each individual taster. Including the fixed effects does not affect the qualitative results, and the coefficients themselves change only slightly. A Wald test rejects that the fixed effects are jointly equal to zero, by a wide margin ($p$-value < 0.001). All of these results apply regardless of whether we use ordered probit or OLS.

To make sure that our results are not driven by wines at the extreme ends of the price range, we also run our regressions on a reduced sample, omitting observations in the top and bottom deciles of the price distribution. Given the broad range of prices in the sample, this is an appropriate precaution. The wines in the reduced sample range in price from $6 to $15.

Using the reduced sample, we estimate Model 2 using both ordered probit and OLS, in each case with and without fixed effects. The qualitative results are highly consistent with those we get when using the full sample. In fact, the effects are larger, and the statistical significance improves further ($p$-value, non-expert price coefficient: 0.001).

# Index of wines

Malenchini Chianti, 193
Man Vintners Cabernet
   Sauvignon, 194
Man Vintners Chenin Blanc,
   195
Mania Rueda, 196
Mark West Pinot Noir, 197
Marqués de Cáceres Rioja, 198
Matua Pinot Noir, 199
Mavrodaphne of Patras,
   Kourtaki, 183
Mediterannean White, René
   Barbier, 221
Mediterranean Red, René
   Barbier, 220
Mélange Noir, Waterbrook, 258
Merlot
   MontAsolo, 202
   Lagaria, 185
   Monthaven, 205
   Washington Hills, 257
Mionetto Il Prosecco, 200
Mohua Sauvignon Blanc, 201
MontAsolo Merlot, 202
Monte Antico, 203
Montecillo Rioja Crianza, 204
Monthaven Merlot, 205
Nobilo Sauvignon Blanc, 206
Norton Cabernet Sauvignon,
   207
Norton Malbec, 208
Oggi Pinot Grigio, 209
Old Vine Zin, Bogle, 113
Opala Vinho Verde, 210
Oro de Castilla, 211
Oyster Bay Sauvignon Blanc,
   212
Parducci Sustainable Red, 213
Pascual Toso Malbec, 214

Petite Sirah
   Bogle, 114
Concannon, 139
Pinot Grigio
   Cycles Gladiator, 143
   Hogue Cellars, 174
   Oggi, 209
Pinot Gris, Villa Wolf, 252
Pinot Noir
   Bogle, 115
   Cycles Gladiator, 144
   Jacob's Creek Reserve, 181
   Mark West, 197
   Matua, 199
   Robert Mondavi, 222
   Turning Leaf, 245
Pölka Dot Riesling, 215
Principessa Gavia , 216
Prosecco, Borgo Magredo Extra
   Dry, 119
Prosecco, Zardetto, 262
Quinta da Aveleda Vinho Verde,
   217
Quinta da Cabriz, 218
Quinta da Romeira, 219
René Barbier Mediterranean
   Red, 220
René Barbier Mediterranean
   White, 221
Riesling
   Columbia Crest Two Vines,
   137
   Dr. L, 152
   Estancia, 156
   Pölka Dot, 215
   Targovishte, 239
Rioja
   Campo Viejo, 121
   Cortijo, 142